*L*EAVETAKINGS

By Corinna Cook

LEAVETAKINGS

By Corinna Cook

ALASKA
LITERARY
SERIES

Text © 2020 University of Alaska Press

Published by
University of Alaska Press
P.O. Box 756240
Fairbanks, AK 99775-6240

Cover and inxterior design by 590 Design.

Cover art by Hollis Kitchin, "Mountain Love" watercolor on paper 2018.
Copyright 2018 all rights reserved, used with permission, www.holliskitchin.com

Names have been changed in "Tending to Bread" and "Confetti"
to respect individuals' privacy.

Earlier versions of certain essays appeared in the following publications:
"Tending to Bread," *Flyway—Journal of Writing and Environment*
"Confetti," *Alaska Quarterly Review*
"The Funeral," *Nowhere Magazine*
"Otter Meditation," *Animal*
"The Cut," *Ocean State Review*

Library of Congress Cataloging-in-Publication Data

Names: Cook, Corinna Jo, author.
Title: Leavetakings / by Corinna Cook.
Description: Fairbanks, AK : University of Alaska Press, [2020]
Identifiers: LCCN 2019058779 (print) | LCCN 2019058780 (ebook) |
ISBN 9781602234246 (paperback) | ISBN 9781602234253 (ebook)
Subjects: LCSH: Cook, Corinna Jo—Travel—Alaska. | Natural
History—Alaska. | Nature—Effect of human beings on—Alaska. | Human
Ecology—Alaska. | Alaska—Description and travel. |
Alaska—Environmental conditions.
Classification: LCC F910.5 .C657 2020 (print) |
LCC F910.5 (ebook) | DDC 917.9804—dc23
LC record available at https://lccn.loc.gov/2019058779
LC ebook record available at https://lccn.loc.gov/2019058780

For T&G and
Muskeg Gulch

CONTENTS

INLAND

A TRAVERSE

I leave the limestone bluffs of North America's middle to take a straight line west across the breadbasket. It is early summer. When the western edge of Nebraska begins behaving like the high desert of Wyoming, I understand flatness in the Great Plains is deceptive: the whole shield of earth tilts so that without noticing, I've climbed at least four thousand feet. It means the air on the western side of Nebraska is thinner than at its eastern edge. I breathe deeply, trying to taste this air and detect the new absence, the new emptiness around me. High in the sky is a bald eagle. As I'm not expecting something so familiar, so intimate, so soon, the eagle sets off the strangeness of our surroundings. Scrubby brush. Hot bright sky. Monoculture on the other side of the road. I am small in the flat wind and wonder if the eagle is well, if it has what it needs.

I push into Wyoming's sage country and cross it south to north. The dog, Pep, and I hike in the Bighorn Mountains and their great layers of red and purple and yellow rock: ancient seafloors, part and parcel of the Rockies. These I follow through Montana, into British Columbia, and then into Alberta. Farther north, the steep sedimentary mountains will flatten into an inland expanse of basaltic plains underlying a swampy boreal forest. The road will turn west into a cluster of

3

peaks at the edge of the British Columbia–Yukon border and continue across the Liard Plain, the Cassiar Mountains, and the Yukon Plateau. When the road reaches the mountainous Coastal Belt, it will climb for a good spell and then drop into Alaska's Saint Elias Mountains and the rainforest at the edge of the sea alongside which I was born.

It is a four-thousand-mile route and a distance more logically traversed by plane. But I want more time. I want to see that distance more clearly. The dog and I take the pickup truck; we have designs to go north in May, south in August. It is this simple. I am crossing the continent to look at the shape of it.

Of the continent: it's unbelievable that road infrastructure overlays so much of it. Unbelievable that a whole plate of the earth's crust has a net of asphalt threads laid atop it. Unbelievable, the nonchalance this creates. Crossing the continent to see its shape is less an expedition and more a comfortable contemplation. I will ford no rivers. I will search for passage through the mountains not for survival, but simply to walk Pep, study the game trails, and enjoy wayfinding on unfamiliar ground.

I will watch the continent change as I go north in early spring. Then in late summer, I will watch it change in reverse. It is important to go both directions. It takes repetitions to see where you've been. And things look different when you're leaving—even the air is different. Often, what I'm leaving is Alaska, though in my heart I am never absent from the place and my departures probably reflect more obscure schisms. At least the place is a marker, clear enough that I can count the days until I return. When the number is small, I announce it. *Dog!* I say. *We're going back!* She knows exactly where.

I worry about the eagle in Nebraska because the ones I know live so well and so differently. They gorge on spawning salmon when the fish come in. They build enormous nests weighing easily a ton. Yet along Nebraska's interstate there are no salmon streams to promise feasting abundance. There is no tree that could support the nests of eagles I know. How can this creature flourish here? I know that as a raptor of the plains and prairie, it was never meant to live identically to its relatives of the northern rainforested coast. And I should have respect for that, for the dignity of the prairie dwellers among the species. But I feel I've glimpsed this eagle across a morbid gulf, one of time and change: the Great Plains wasn't always a place of industrial agriculture. That dark-winged eagle making its high circles above mechanically cultivated, chemically curated land—does it carry generational memories of prairie grasses, of bison herds? Is its resilience here also a kind of mourning? I feel my destination would suit this eagle, that we ought both seek refuge in the north. *You can come with me,* I offer, and watch it circling until it is a dot, and then gone.

For the eagle's resilience on overcultivated land, I can take no credit; for my own journey across and away from this same land, I owe many debts and bear layers of complicity. Offered free acreage and citizenship in the nineteenth century, government-invited migrants took root on this continent, and I am their progeny, descended from Germans-become-Americans who homesteaded here in Nebraska. My personal lineage on this continent thus includes the displacement of Plains Indians and the linked transformation of open prairie into parceled farmland. History, politics, materiality, and family connect me to the massive agro-industrial complex I've had the privilege to largely avoid, and alongside which this eagle lives every day.

My parents moved to Alaska in the seventies. It was a good time and place to be young, poor, and educated. On my mom's first trip, she delighted in Anchorage's Quonset huts. She liked it there. On my dad's first trip, his ferry money ran out in Petersburg so he found a job, lived on break room cookies until payday, then got back on the ferry and headed to Glacier Bay for a kayak trip. He liked it there too. They each wrapped up law school down south and together moved into a cabin on the beach by Lawson Creek on Douglas Island. It was a shack and a palace all in one. By the time I was born, they'd moved a few miles out North Douglas, off the beach and onto the uphill side of the road where they've lived in the forest ever since.

I want to go back slowly this time, do it in a pickup truck instead of a Boeing 747. Go look at the large ancient continent—it will cut worries down to size, make problems small. The problem of aging, for example. My favorite folk, those belonging to the circle that raised me up, are graying and silvering in the rainy, mountainous, stolen land we love. It lends a particular chill to the distance yawning between me and the hearth around which my people nightly gather. I clink my glass to theirs every evening I am there. And I think the clink of their glasses every other evening in the lonesome ear of my mind.

I'll take some time and miles to detach, I tell those who ask about my trip. *Reflect on what I've missed these past years. Reflect on what I've shied away from. Reflect on what I'll place at the center of the next ones.*

I have always been curious about things that get sewn up together and the things people put into one story. Belonging, parents, and the circle of lifelong friends that are family—I'm sewing these to an easy journey across the continental crust. I'm sewing them to an expanse of rock overlaid with a thin asphalt weave of roads.

If roads are like a fabric upon the land, its weave is all knotted up in metropolitan areas. Where the mesh is loose, the land shows through. Over parts of Wyoming or the Dakotas, for example, the road network thins out and the people are fewer and farther between. And here and there over the continent the mesh finally frays or disintegrates entirely. People call these places "remote" or "the backcountry." But edge your view of the continent toward the subarctic: one or two roads traverse this whole expanse, but there's no weave, no mesh. They trail from the hem of the road system, stray threads draped across the earth's northern crust.

That will come soon. For now I'm following the Rockies across the US-Canada border. Early in the Canadian Rockies I make an impulse buy, acquiring *Geology of British Columbia*, an updated 2014 edition with new color-plated photographs. I am looking at the shape of the continent after all. *Less gravitas, less gravitas*, chants my spirit. *More breeziness.* Less gravitas, indeed. I will learn the rocks! Problems in the circle of life are more manageable when I tend to the sturdiest materials underfoot. Rocks remind me the world is large and old and was set down slowly in layers.

Geology of British Columbia may be updated with new color-plated photographs, but it's not easy bedtime reading. Tonight I'm underlining as best I can, though the page and pen angles don't suit the way I've zipped myself into my sleeping bag. This headlamp is dim, and I keep mixing up the NAb and NAp notations from the chart of ancestral North American terranes.

The bigger picture is that weathering produces erosion here, deposition there. Currents under the earth's crust float continents around atop magma. They rub; they crash; they separate. They fragment. They suture and combine. Unfathomably, continental plates even *smear*, a verb geologists use without flinching. In fact, much of my own biome, the Alexander Archipelago, is made from crustal plates of overheated clays that split from Eurasia, went rafting over the North Pole, and got smeared one by one along the basaltic continental margin of western Canada and the United States.

Much later the ice age did its work in this region. I think back and see glacial tongues licking the ears of all the rocks, sculpting in them an unerring allegiance to the ice. What exists now is fjord country, where the slopes are as steep above the water line as they are below it and the pumping of the tide twice daily scrubs all the channels and inlets beneath peaks where snow, up high, holds to the rock year-round.

That's where I'm headed.

It's where my mom taught me to glance around for bears when I got off the school bus with my clarinet. It's where my stay-at-home dad raised me speaking, singing, joking, reading, and writing in French—not his language by birth or nationality, but his by choice—for French met his Anglo mind and mouth with something delectable, savory, and ultimately irreplaceable. In any case, I'm headed to the place where my mom taught me—with humor and sincerity—that running away from problems works just fine, the place where my dad taught me how to follow any watershed to the beach if I lost the trail. My parents have a multivalent respect for loneliness and risk-taking and contemplation, things to which I had, they felt, a basic and limitless right.

It's morning in the Rockies and I wouldn't trade their piney smell for anything. I'm on the shoulder of the smooth road, leaning silently out my truck's open window or perhaps sitting in the open window itself, upper body outside the truck, arm slung over the roof of the cab, feet resting inside on the driver's seat. I've joined a small row of parked, worshipful folk—are we gathered with a hush before an elk? A group of bighorns? There is so much wildlife in the park, I can't remember whose hooves scraped the earth or what shape snout flared its nostrils at the moment I see an asymmetry in the reflection cast by my truck onto the rear window of the car ahead. Asymmetry means I have an out headlight. *S'okay don't need it,* I think. *Won't be dark again till August, September. Don't need it.*

A couple days later I leave. It's early morning.

The land flattens. There is a light fog. I see a caribou in the white-gray air and pull over to spend time with it, hear the rustle-click of its steps, see what it's eating. Caribou seem weightless when they move. The one I'm watching doesn't flinch when an eighteen-wheeler roars by, but still it disappears, springing on hooves so light even the fog remains still. The whoosh following the semi rocks my truck: the driver didn't slow down, didn't edge into the other lane to give me space. I understand I shouldn't pull over here. The parks are a gentle exception, but in the north, the road does not generally belong to reverie. It belongs to industry.

In 2006 I was a college student with a summer research stipend. I used it to gather perspectives on a potential copper and gold mining project—then in active exploration phases— called Pebble Mine. The basic background I learned about Pebble was that when or if dug, it would be the biggest open pit mine in North America, its tailings dam would become the largest dam in the world, and hauling ore would require both the construction of a deepwater port in Cook Inlet and the construction of a ninety-mile access road linking the port to the mine—a mine that would sit near Lake Iliamna, at the

headwaters of Bristol Bay. This information was widely available, repeated across many accessible publications, and carried varying degrees of irrelevance to my own discoveries. For
what I learned in my personal conversations was that whether
someone wanted or didn't want the mine, memories from the
cruelest moments of their lives were mashed up in what they
had to say about excavating those rocks.

"The headwaters of Bristol Bay" is a heavy phrase. It means
this: the headwaters of Alaska's most important salmon
fishery. These are the fish that feed the forest, that feed the
animals, the people. These are the fish that make all of us relatives. In all the carriages of all our bodies we ride the steady
silver ocean throb.

My project in 2006 was to trace the shape of the debate. I
asked people what was going on and what they thought, and I
listened to how they talked about it. In Anchorage I recorded
interviews, sat in offices, took tours, accepted bumper stickers, and chatted in elevators. Then I went out to Bristol Bay's
headwaters region. There I took mail planes between villages,
hitchhiked from airstrips, conversed, listened, walked dirt
roads, walked over tundra, looked at fish, looked at rocks.
Watched the creeks flow with spawning sockeye, watched the
salmon close-up as they nosed the stones, fanning their gills.
I also watched the salmon from small planes. From the sky,
fish look dense and dark, packed in like ants as they follow
the threads of their creek-trails. Flying over, you can see how
crowded a creek is the same way that from a jet, you can see
how crowded a city's highways are.

When I visited the central mining exploration site in the
village of Iliamna, I saw carpenters sawing and nailing plywood wings to a series of heavy objects slated to be lifted by

helicopter. I watched a wooden outhouse lift off. With its fresh plywood wings, the outhouse rose into the air straight and true—no spinning at the end of its cable, no dangerous pendulum swing from the belly of the chopper. Whoever made those wings even painted them with a few black curves to suggest wing feathers.

When I started the project, I was trying on policy. I thought one day I would work in natural resources. But the Pebble conversation struck me as senseless. I felt tossed away, for both the mining project's supporters and its critics treated precisely the same facts as the bedrock of opposite conclusions. In this sense, there was no debate at all—I found instead that an impasse divided fundamentally disconnected ideologies, that the real divisions were deeply buried and largely unvoiced, and that a head-on policy approach thus missed both the depth and the complex silences at the heart of the disagreement. And so I changed from policy to art. In the arts I sought a more roundabout mode of inquiry, or points of entry that would draw much closer to the heart of my questions by following Emily Dickinson's advice to "tell all the truth but tell it slant." More specifically, that is when I began a search—one that continues—for a kind of ethnography capable of mapping the odd mixture of humor and holiness and love and irony that moves a person to paint wing feathers on plywood so that bound across the tundra, a shithouse will fly straight.

A mail plane took me to the other side of Lake Iliamna, where the water edges mountains. It dropped me off in the village of Pedro Bay, population forty-two. I met a large black and white dog there, Oreo, who walked many miles with me over the course of several days. One morning he walked me to the Tribal Council Headquarters. And he was waiting when I emerged several hours later, already rising to his feet as I stepped out the door and into the fine rain. Oreo had no questions. He simply took me as his charge. To him I owe a great debt. There were villages in which I was not permitted to walk freely. Bear country, and other reasons. Good ones. But in Pedro Bay the people trusted Oreo, and Oreo's oversight allowed me to wander, make my small discoveries, sip the air.

My philosophy is, rely on the dog. The dog's senses go far; the dog always knows. Oreo's patient vigilance was a great courtesy and a gift I could not reciprocate. But it was also more than that. It was an induction, consummating my link to a region in which I neither grew up nor properly lingered. I left with a baffling sense of accountability, another complicated debt.

Beware the poetics of juxtaposition. Here coexist large-scale mechanized infrastructure governed by capitalism and vast, vast ecosystems governed by organic processes. These two poles both take up a lot of space, and if enormity has charisma, opposite enormities have all the more.

And beware the related and kind of fantastical disjunction riddling the north. Heavy industry coexists with living tradition, with lifeways both contemporary and ancient at once. I remember the mining company's human relations person explaining their local hire policy was a bust, *We send company pickup trucks to wake them up in the morning because they're not used to shift work*, she told me. *We even pack them sandwiches.* She pushed on the word *sandwiches*. I still remember her voice. They had to recruit, fly in, and house many workers from out of state because so many Bristol Bay locals, even many who *want* to work for the mining exploration sites, disappear. I remember nodding, as I had been nodding throughout my conversation with the human relations person. *They go hunting*, I prompted, and she shrieked, because that was exactly it, and she could not fathom.

Finally, beware the hypervisibility of heavy industry's inherent problems. For example, part of what oil engineers do to keep the industry's infrastructure working is to design retrofits and new plans, including elevated drill rigs, to account for the melting ice caps, rising sea level, and loss of permafrost their own scientists predicted—to a T—in the seventies. In the north, this is no abstraction. Buildings sit on this melting permafrost, requiring frequent adjustment to remain level. Villages fall into the sea where the shoreline, no longer protected by sea ice year-round, is laid bare to erosion by summer storms.

I am, like so many, enraged. I am enraged by the simplest facts of the system and by the depth of my complicity in it.

But I designed my travel on the road neither as confrontation nor denunciation; I try to remember my purpose now is more contemplative. I am not studying a mineral deposit so vast it is yet to be fully delineated, a deposit underlying grief and resilience and ferocity so vast it, too, may be unmapped. No, on this trip I just wish to glimpse the shape of the continent. I am simply trying to see something I am too small to see. This is, I believe, a perfectly normal human endeavor.

John McPhee writes about doing a similar trip latitudinally across America's contiguous forty-eight. Road cuts, explains McPhee, give particular and eerie access to cross-sections of continental crust. And our road system is the most extensive in human history. "We as geologists are fortunate to live in a period of great road building," one expert tells McPhee—because anyone, really, can take a coast-to-coast look at the rocks.

Gratitude casts odd shadows when we perceive the strangeness of the phenomenon, though. For McPhee also quotes another geologist, Karen Kleinspehn, who sees I-80 and roads like it as violence, albeit a blip of civilization. In Kleinspehn's eyes, interstates are bizarre, temporary, and darkly fascinating.

> This interstate is like a knife wound all across the country. . . . A person or two. One car. Coast to coast. People do it now without thinking much about it. Yet it's a most unusual kind of personal freedom—particular to this time span, the one we happen to be in. It's an amazing, temporary phenomenon that will end. We have the best highway system in the world. It lets us do what people in no other country can do. And it's an ecological disaster.

I read very little of McPhee's book. I do not really want to think about roads. I've grasped his project, I've tasted his approach, so I move on. Yet confidence in moving on is, in my experience, an easy sign to miss.

In the first days of my journey I don't yet see the shape of the continent as it sits between the middle west of America and the north, but I do see how "the road" changes substantially from here to there. Grids of precise geometry parcel up the Midwest. You drive in straight lines, make ninety-degree turns. You pass pleasant towns of pleasant folk at even intervals with many upstanding rows of corn between them. But the road in the north is anomalous, jerky. Small and thin. Vein-like, perhaps. Vital and inconsequential at once.

If this great net of asphalt cast over the continent—tightly woven into many interlocking grids over one region, a loose thread or two trailing upon another—is part of "an amazing, temporary phenomenon that will end," it is also a reminder that the underlying rock of the continent itself already connects its most distant lands. Road system notwithstanding, a bug could walk from one to another any day it pleases.

Yet for now there are roads—and there is *a* road—from here to there, from that world to this. There is asphalt the whole way. This is both democratic and a severe limitation. Democratic because in a driving culture the road means access, free and open. And a severe limitation because reliance is a tether. To the extent you rely on the road, you are tethered to asphalt.

I am conscious of this for various reasons. Among them is that my hometown is not on a road system. Juneau is edged with sea and forest and a fifteen-hundred-square-mile ice field. When I was in high school, we traveled for the regional honor music festival by ferry and went to All-State and All-Northwest by plane. Once a year the pep band and cheerleading squad would travel together to the regional basketball tournament, filling an entire ferry with teenagers, instrument cases, and pom-poms. Cheerleaders and band kids would work on math together while watching for orcas during ten- to thirty-hour sailings.

We are hardly homogenous. Those of us who grew up this way have a diverse range of home lives and outside experiences. But even the most cosmopolitan among us do not take interminably connective, cross-country roadways for granted. We are all shaped by a rainy and proud and complicated town that wears no asphalt leash.

Long-distance driving thus intrigues and repels me. Yes, I am using roads to cross the continent. Yet I take our nation's Blues Elders seriously and always remember that crossroads are the liminal space of the devil and that "going up the highway" means dying.

It is some hours after I've left the Canadian Rockies. A good spell has passed since I've stopped to watch the caribou. I've understood the shoulder was not built for my stopping; out of respect for that realization I've put in some miles traversing Alberta. But at this moment the dog and I are on foot trekking—stupidly—outside the guardrail inches off the shoulder of a remote single-lane road on which semis are doing eighty, on a hill, and a curve, in light fog, dusted by late spring snowflakes.

Here the road comes around the side of a mountain, and the loose rock of the embankment I'm trying to walk on is too steep for safety, too high for comfort. But I swear I've just seen a coal mine. Yes, look, there's a whole coal mine down there. I have to photograph it. There's more black rock than I've ever seen. An expanse of buildings and trucks and conveyor belts and chutes and cisterns and culverts and scaffolding, all built on terrain sculpted into the black rock. Terraces, parking pads, building foundations sculpted into the black rock. Linked up with its own local road system sculpted into the black rock. I am trekking back along this road overlooking the coal mine because there was no way to stop the car, no place to pull over, and I have to photograph this. Or maybe I just have to look at it, do a double-take. Or is it that I have to remember something, change my life, receive a sign from the undead. I don't even know what I have to do.

The dog does not like the high, loose terrain outside the guardrail. She does not like the eighteen-wheelers clanging by. I curse. I am not here to "look" at industry. I've stopped at no oil fields. I've interviewed no frackers. Pored over no Canadian Geologic Survey maps. Been escorted into no company housing trailers, descended into no mineshafts, sat in on no safety meetings. Because industry is not my project. This should suffice to send me on my way, find someplace pretty, set up camp, stomp my feet against the cold, concentrate on being a good guest in bear country—anything other than mull over the complicated grief of extraction.

In the end of course it is the dog, her overly delicate steps and the alarm in her eyes that release me. Every time she touches her nose to my calf, I've been telling her sweet things and pushing farther along this hairy top lip over a gullet of coal. But she is trembling, and I know it. She is such a good dog. *We don't have to stay with the coal mine any longer,* I finally tell her, and she does an immediate 180, bounding back from where we came. Rely on the dog.

Here is the paradox, the discovery. Geology is a lullaby in low elephant pitches. Its poetics of ancientness and enormity and transformation are soothing. But geology also guides extraction, the surgical component of earth science. And my knowledge of extraction is that it's sewn up with grief. Leaving the coal mine, I am pensive.

It doesn't last. I have an out headlight, driver's side. It's a touch foggy. *Low ceiling,* we say. Spring is late; little snowflakes swirl. They're hard to see through, but they're also a warning that it might be cold enough for the fog's moisture to freeze. Probably some patches of black ice on the road.

I am accustomed to slowing down in conditions. Par for the course. But I am sharing the road with logging trucks, coal trucks, oil riggers, and unidentifiable industry affiliates. I am sharing the road with laborers racing to beat company time. Their loads can swing. I am crossing a no-nonsense workplace far from regulatory oversight or medical aid, and I'm doing it with only one headlight.

I'm writing about my own blindness.

But the dangers in this moment are physical; I am not thinking about the shape of the continent anymore. I am not trying to grasp that flattening I witnessed, but can't believe, from the Rockies to the plains. I am only gripping the wheel. Going slow. Hugging the white line. Hollering *I exist!* every time headlights brighten the fog ahead. Murmuring *see me, see me seemeseemeseeme*. Cursing to rinse out the fear every time a semi jerks and swerves with surprise, revealing it's noticed my little pickup only in the moment of being upon it.

The land I'm crossing through snow flurries is a huge expanse of tight wiry conifers, dry rootballs overlaid with mosses, lichens, and Labrador tea. There is this forest, then suddenly burning flames atop towers three times taller than any tree. Forest, then the metronomic pump jacks in an oil field. Forest, then sodden gravel pads of identical trailer industry housing, lights brightening not one window. Every few miles, another ruler-straight dirt road cuts the forest to link the highway with another site of industry. The hours I spend traversing all this are slow and tense and defeating. Then there is a sudden change.

In Canada's plains of boreal forest sits a sore place, paved. At latitude fifty-five Highway 40 swells to several lanes. Hotel chains blossom. Franchises proliferate. Logos stand against the sky. Grande Prairie, Alberta, where I lose the road to Alaska. Illogically, I wonder if anyone else has ever been here. Are there legends? Of crossing the forested, industrialized plains and then entering a city of box stores? More logically, I wonder if anyone has ever rolled into Grande Prairie and *not* lost the road to Alaska. The city is overpaved. The road could be anywhere.

From where I am, halfway up the province of Alberta, it's another eighty miles to get to that road. We call it the Alcan, the 1942 Alaska-Canada Highway. But I am caught in the swollen lanes and boxy franchises and all the steel poles with their crow's nest panels of corporate advertising. Strings of plastic triangle flags hang in arcs, pointing in wan colors at the pavement.

The beacon of a car dealership sign, when it appears, offers strange solace. It isn't the way to the Alcan, but it will do for the headlight. I change lanes. Signal left. Find a man, Brad, in the fluorescent hum of the sales department. Now my voice is loud, my face windburned, my clothes lived-in, slept-in, hiked-in, unchanged for a week. In other words, I am well. But for this episode among the box stores, I am well. Brad can see it in my sound. My words are flushed pink from forward motion and leave clear turquoise in their wake. Right away I like him because he speaks in colors too, in grounded golden-brown, and when he understands I have lost the road, he laughs. There is only one road. It is true. There is only one. *I know*, I tell him. Together our colors look like a pale dawn over the earth's spring thaw. We are rising to the occasion of our meeting, immediately friends.

Thank you for trucking around the dealership, thank you for petting my dog, thank you for photographing the VIN and for finding the part. Thank you for the staged joke you have with the front desk guy in Parts and Services. I laughed as I reached for my credit card, and really this is very smart: you two have a funny thing you say to lighten the mood at the moment of paying that renders the paying painless. Thank you for then pulling a mechanic off a scheduled job, thank you later for walking back out with me, having me start the truck, and thumbs-upping the new driver's side headlight. Thank you for printing a map at your office desk and highlighting my neon way out of Grande Prairie, Alberta.

19

We are speaking in colors, sweeping along in an exchange that is really a painting that is really a mirror of the land when I ask Brad about Canada's 150th anniversary year. It is a casual question, light. And this is what he says of the 150 years: his grandpa was ninety-five. A 150 years is only a generation more than his grandpa. His country's just starting out. *My grandpa was ninety-five,* he says again, leaning into something brittle.

Mine was ninety-two. I would like to say so because I can tell Brad's grandpa is dead and that the bruise holds every purple there is. I want him to know mine is, too, and that this bruise also goes all the way down. But I say nothing because abruptly he has departed on a colorless search for the right words. I have a squeeze of sadness at this. My new friend, launching a rowboat on punchy seas, cranking his oars to go alone into this other way of speaking. One that struggles. That tries to do right by everything he holds dear. That can't.

Yet I respect that he takes the question seriously. It is a serious question to me, too. A 150 is a round-number benchmark in the history of the settler state. A good time for grave discussion.

Instead there is a party. And there are party favors. For example, the government offers free entry to the country's national parks all year. The park pass hooked to my truck's rearview mirror is dark green with a golden beaver. No mixed feelings on this particular point. I'm grateful for the welcome into protected public lands. *Kootenay,* I say at some point. *Banff. Jasper.* But these places aren't prominent on the maps Brad keeps next to his heart; they don't give us traction. What he says is that his grandpa was ninety-five. And that his country's just starting out.

Brad in his leather jacket. His fitted copper-khaki pants. His search for the right words. His hometown is an hour and a half north of Grande Prairie. His hometown, he says, is *where there's work in the oil fields or there's work in the oil fields*. He searches me to see if I understand. I want to honor his pause. But I should own my narrowness; in truth I have always had options. So I strain to hear. Brad's voice drops. He is neither resentful nor superior. He comes from where there's work in the oil fields or there's work in the oil fields, and while he left that place, everyone who shaped him works in those fields.

Within the hour and a half from here to there he must traverse many powerful boundaries, real and imagined, to visit home. If he is proud, it is not a pride in departure, for he took his leave and lives with the loneliness of it.

I am ashamed of phrases I've landed on in my mind, ashamed of my plans to record this place in my notebook as "another mistake of the industrialized West," or simply, "a dump of a strip mall town." I am ashamed this mind of mine was scripting his dismissal.

Brad's honesty and vulnerability set in motion a whole new exchange. Its terms are more complicated. For one, now I will remember him. And I will think about what he's sewn up into one story. As listener, I'll feel strangely sewn into the story as well. And I'll wonder what forms of reciprocity this is already drawing from me, feeding swift currents neither of us can chart.

I leave Grande Prairie, and it is a mistake I don't understand. I drive hard, and I get as far as a very clean, kept up, golf-cart-monitored campground. Maybe I make dinner there, but it is certain I don't stay long. Campgrounds aren't my habit; I prefer to rough it. I keep driving. And thinking. We had been talking in colors. Then we were alone in our rowboats. Something's not right and I'll either outrun it or catch up to it, but all of my cells know the answer is to go on down the road in the pale northern night.

It is a broad sky glowing rose over frozen, muddy taiga, roadside patches of snow dirty with industrial traffic. I drive until my eyes will not read the road so that dimly I know I've got to sleep. I've gone too far. I'm loopy and I'm nodding off, but it's cold. "Services" and people in general have grown fewer and farther between, and this is the wrong place for a mistake. I wish I was a mollusk. A bivalve. I want a strong shell suctioned shut where I can seal in with my own perfect juices.

I turn off on a muddy, ruler-straight road. It could go anywhere, a mine, a dump site, who knows. I just mean to get a ways off the pavement and turn off the engine. I'll put on every piece of clothing I have, shiver in my sleeping bag, and doze as my breath freezes to my lashes. I try to keep my wits about me, pay attention to the mud. How deep is it? Am I going to get stuck? Will the tires freeze into the glop overnight? Obviously they will, but can I handle this with some fierce kicking? Or am I out of my league? With springtime, dirt roads liquefy surface-first. If the road's still frozen four inches down, I should be fine. If the mud soup is deeper than that, there could be problems.

The mud soup is definitely deeper than that.

Out of nowhere comes a huge green pickup truck. It dwarfs mine, plowing through the mud slowly like a ship. The thin ice just forming at the surface of the mud shatters evenly before those slow tires. It sounds like cellophane. The truck is packed full of people, faces watching me. No one raises a hand. No one smiles. No one blinks. The ship of the truck passes, is gone. They've got all the information they need. I'm a woman. I'm alone. My own truck is the little gray one with a boat rack on the roof, easy to recognize. Not that there are any other travelers passing through with winter snow still on the ground.

I've lived a very easy life: just enough sorrow to know things are more volatile than I grasp, less predictable than I can help, more straight-up violent than I realize.

It's really cold. I drove too long and can't think straight. Can I stay here? It would be a gamble.

There was a roadside *something* a few miles back. I resolve to go back to it, park in their muddy lot for a few hours. It's on the edge of the road and uncomfortably visible, but there's no privacy elsewhere anyway. Too far north for much darkness. Taiga trees are small. Not going to drive any distance down a mud-slop industry access road and get myself stuck. If I'm parked at a building, however ramshackle, I'll look at least plausibly like I belong. Even if the place is padlocked and deserted. But I hope someone is there. Runs a business. Holds their own peace; keeps their own order. Again I drive.

Better if it had been deserted, though. Instead a man with long yellow teeth appears, warning me of Jesus. I nod once in acknowledgment and sidestep, begin to explain there is a truck of people that stared me down, and since I need to sleep I wonder if—but already he is waving his arms: *There's no camping!* he shouts. *You don't have Jesus in your heart, you'll be eaten by bears!* Bears will rip into my truck. It is no better than tinfoil. Despite myself, I take a step back. But he takes a step forward, and we're locked in to that dance of politeness and power, threat and deflection. His long teeth are remarkable. It's still cold. I still drove too long, and I still can't think straight.

How do I end up on Pink Mountain? By pushing through more of the night, the pale-lit non-night of exhausted night, feeling angry and fierce and fragile.

Especially feeling fragile.

The next thing I find are some rows of industry trailer housing frozen hard into the spring muck at the foot of a rise in the land. I understand the green pickup truck came from here or from a place like it, so I can't pull in to industry housing. I have to stay on the road, which now swings up the slope of the rise, a symmetric, topographic bulge in the swampy boreal forest of the basaltic plains. This is Pink Mountain. It is not a mountain at all, but a formation geologists call a *dome*. Neither destination nor refuge, Pink Mountain looks me in the eye of my memory and smirks.

At the apex of the dome's bulge are a couple businesses in various degrees of disarray. They may or may not be open so early in the spring. There is a fuel pump. There are some trailers. Looks pretty snowed in, but somehow this is also a campground. There is a convenience store, wooden and weathered, sagging into the mud. Permafrost must be melting unevenly under the foundation. Middle of the night, but it's open. In I go.

Two workers in huge industry overalls with huge industry boots are buying beef jerky and chewing tobacco, openly scrolling through porn on their phones. I say a quiet *heya*. They do not smile or speak. Their eyes flick from me to their screens and back, thumbs hovering over lit images of flesh and curves and hair. And they do not move, though I would like a turn at the counter as well. They must live in industry trailer housing either near here or far from here. They must have worked hard this winter. They must be beloved to somebody. But they stroke their screens and watch me and I feel that anything could provoke anyone and there would be no warning before and no more than a yawn afterward. My helplessness and I pay for a campsite. We pick our way out and don't exhale till we've stepped through the door, where our breath makes a white cloud and shields us from nothing.

What's not snow is mud. What's not mud is snow. I gauge campsites by the protruding picnic tables and jam the truck into the snow in hopes of remaining afloat above the sludge. Not far is a Minnesota-plated RV, my neighbor for the night. I don't want to meet its driver or any of its passengers. I just hope they care if I scream.

Breath freezing to my face, down bag cinched tight up to my nose, winter coat thrown over the dog as she shivers in her dog bed, I allow myself zero thoughts. I am a mollusk. I am a bivalve. No thinking; no entry.

What's hostile, unpredictable, vengeful, and especially preda-tory at one, or two, or three in the morning can dissipate a few hours later. The change is probably illusory. But this morning as I am shivering it's a change that permits me to throw on my down jacket, stuff my fists into my pockets, and look around. It permits me to tromp a few minutes through the dwarf dome-top trees, gather myself. Reclaim a bit of mental quietude.

Postholing in the black ice–plated sludge of mud of mid-forest industrial Canada, I stop to watch the dog raise her nose, make her silent inquiry. A pause. Then she is satisfied. By what? We trudge on and find a pile of old tires. They are heavy machinery tires, each one bigger in diameter than I am tall, a pell-mell mountain dwarfing the surrounding trees. The dog sniffs. I gaze. Soon we will leave Pink Mountain, relieved to owe a goodbye to nobody but also disappointed by the same. No one marked the arrival, except by exchange of cash over an ill-lit counter. No one will mark the departure.

Being unaccounted for cuts both ways. I think of Brad's young country, how it pushed him out of his family home in the oil fields and into the strip mall scab in the midst of forest. I think of his grandpa, of whom he speaks in past tense yet also invokes as explanation for the present. I think of Brad's loyalty, how it's nailed to memory of his grandpa, how that memory gathers and measures the world, gives him the footing from which to reckon with the day.

I wonder if he'd recognize this picture of himself. Does Brad see himself this way? Or is he actually living trackless and traceless, departing from memory of his grandfather and returning, oddly, haphazardly, simply taking an unexpected question seriously, finding himself yet again alongside his grandpa in his mind? Returning though he knows all too well that he's left?

It's mid-May. It's spring in a place where the land's memory of winter is strong. I'll be driving out well before breakfast, well before anyone else awakens. Eventually the day will open behind me; the sky will go from rose to blue. Later, summer will come. People—southerners—will begin trickling through; I'm ahead of the RV roadtripping curve, but it'll follow soon enough. Visitors will come, then they'll go, and then the days will zip up tight into fall. That's when the swampy land all around will blush once, hard, a quick bright red before the snow. I don't even know if you like winter. I do. It's very quiet. That's what will come next.

INTERTIDAL

A RETURN IN
THREE CHAPTERS

CHAPTER ONE

*T*hey insist from the first that I become an athlete. In the winter they strap little skis to my feet, and in the summer they plop my round bottom in a kayak. In all seasons, determined I will learn to catch, they toss koosh balls at me.

I am not opposed to any of these things, but what comes naturally is rescuing earthworms off the shoulder of the road where we live. When we leave the house to walk the dogs, I squat at the bottom of the driveway, trap a fat pink worm with my fat pink baby fingers, and deposit it a few feet off in the ditch. A moment later, I squat again, trapping another fat pink worm with my fat pink fingers, cooing to it about looking left and looking right in case of cars. I do not skip any worms, ever.

CHAPTER TWO

Cyrano de Bergerac is a fine poem. It is also a play, but first it is a fine poem. In fact it is such a fine poem that as a drifting twenty-something with a jug of tears at the back of my throat, I flew across the state to see my hometown theater troupe perform it. I found that, as usual, my hometown smelled of seashells. And I found that, as usual, the night I arrived my father wanted to lounge in front of the fire drinking génépi and telling me about the dogs while my mother wanted to stay up late feeding me leftovers. I tilted my head every so often to steady the jug of tears at the back of my throat. I sipped génépi. I ate leftovers. My father spoke at great length about the dogs and I stared at him, memorizing his face at this age.

In the morning I found that, as usual, my mother crouched before the woodstove as my father tittered on about the dogs. My mother and father were anxious and happy that their drifting twenty-something was home for a day, but it flustered their routine. And so with one hand on my throat to steady the jug of tears, I gathered up my small family for an ambling dog walk along the beach by the boat launch.

I found that, as usual, my mother walked along watching the gravel beneath her feet. And I found that, as usual, my father strolled along resolutely scanning the sea. There were some whale spouts far out and closer to shore a sea lion, whose breathing made clouds at the water's surface. My father spoke of the dogs and stopped here and there to point at another whale and another sea lion that my mother missed because the gravel held her gaze. The jug of tears grew hot, and I was doubly careful not to spill it as I stooped to pick up a blue-and-black mussel shell. The shell grew warm in my pocket as I moved my thumb around its inner curves.

I found that, as usual, the walk somewhat muted and drowsed my parents. My mother made preparations for a nap. My father put up his feet. And I found that, as usual, the jug of tears at the back of my throat had cooled. Now a vapor, I slipped into the kitchen for tea.

CHAPTER THREE

I find the cupboard stocked with boxes of fruited and spiced organic herbal teas, brand-new and still sealed in clear plastic. I pick a box, slit open its plastic wrapping, and remove a single tea bag. The teas have been selected perhaps weeks in advance, stacked here for my arrival.

I have the singular compulsion to taste all of the new teas right then, that afternoon, enacting the hard edges of love and loneliness in the quiet kitchen as if onstage. Before the eyes of no one, I will crush the blue and black mussel shell, still warm in my pocket, and steep it in the heating kettle. Now I am even compelled to eat the crushed shell and soppy tea leaves, to fill the jug at the back of my throat with boiling tea-shell grit. *Yes,* I think. I'll do exactly this, then dig wormlike, headfirst into the cold dirt outside, claw and gnaw and tunnel underground beneath the road, ears filling with earth, eyes scraping raw: I'll burrow into the sweet dark dirt where no traffic comes from the left, and none comes from the right.

FLUID PLACES

A forested far shore crosses the photograph, tree-top scraggle drawn tight like a black ribbon across the frame. A perfect midline.

Water and sky mirror each other across it. Thick saffron clouds bloom against pale blue on the glass of the water exactly as they do in the depth of the sky. But in the water floats a wooden kayak and in the sky hangs a white contrail.

The photographer sat in this kayak. She snapped a shot of the bow in front of her on the water, shoreline beyond, sky beyond that. Because her kayak has a peaked deck, the center seam running its length makes a vertical line up the frame. She aligned it with the white streak of the contrail; the two verticalities mirror one another. Call and response.

Centering everything, the photographer captured a mathematically precise x-y axis charted directly upon the land.

The photograph is on display at the Alaska State Museum. I am at the museum. Because of the weather—rain pelting ice in a stiff, dark wind—I have come down from the mountain early in the day. At odds with winter (where is the snow?) and at odds with solitude (why always alone on a mountain?), I stop at the museum. Temporarily I abandon my crampons, my dog, and even my headlamp. They sit in the car. (*Dog,* I say to the dog. *You stay. And I'll be back.*) She'll be fine. So will the crampons, the headlamp.

Still, separated from these, I could be anyone.

So I am someone studying a photograph. Studying *this* photograph, perhaps because its two axes strike me as wry. Self-conscious. A centered x-axis of shoreline, a centered y-axis of kayak and contrail—precision here is a set-up, but for what? The composition of the frame is so controlled I imagine the photographer deploying an array of engineering instruments to center the lines with utmost mathematical precision, beeps and dials and lasers measuring, adjusting, counter-adjusting.

Of course that is unlikely, as a kayak has no room for the assemblage of wires and switchboards I imagine.

More likely, it would have gone like this: the photographer pushes off from shore. Paddles for a time. Watches the light change as the northern evening unfurls, slow at this high latitude. Notices a contrail in the sky. Maybe feels a pang. Or maybe not. Considers the visual effect, and lines up her kayak as an echo, a reply, a restatement of that same straight line. Snaps a photo.

It would be an unremarkably gorgeous landscape shot of unremarkably majestic Alaska were it not for the eerie x-y algebraic control of the frame. Reflexively, my head turns. My chin draws an inch back. My eyes narrow.

During this snowless early winter of 2017, I take a quick airplane hop from Juneau to Sitka. The last time I went to Sitka, perhaps five or six years ago, I traveled by ferry. A pal and I strapped our kayaks onto his Subaru, drove onto the ferry in Juneau and off in Sitka, and paddled around in waters I knew not at all, waters my friend knew even less. We camped for a few days but had a weather scare and ended up cold and wet but safe in my uncle Dave's guest room. We watched the pounding rain out the window. Listened to weather advisories on the marine radio. Killed time looking at maps.

This time in Sitka, I arrive with hiking boots instead of a kayak. When I get off the plane I want to shake the airport tension clinging to my hair, my clothes. Uncle Dave understands. He and I take a trudge at low tide out at the end of Harbor Point Road. We train our binoculars on seagulls and trumpeter swans, let our toes grow numb. A high-pressure system has this mountainous coastline locked in a spell of cold and clear. We can see forever, but it's well below freezing, not much above zero, and the skin of the sea has begun to thicken here and there with rafts of slush. The low sun throws a blinding white across the water and a glare on the barely snowcapped mountains. The black muck of low tide shines, frozen beneath our feet.

Sitka's got squid now, Uncle Dave tells me.

I'm watching a single swan who is head-down, bottom-up, tailfeathers skyward, black feet poised like outriggers.

Sitka didn't used to have squid.

Now it does.

The swan I'm watching makes slight adjustments to its upside-down balance. I imagine its snaking white neck curving and jabbing underwater and its flat black bill scooping around in the muck.

The young people go up Silver Bay and jig for them, for squid. Cut them into pieces and freeze them for bait, says Uncle Dave. *Maybe some people just fry them up too. Why not. And humpbacks really go in for the squid. Whales are smart; they're not going to pass up a new food source just because it's new.*

I miss the moment when the swan rights itself. Maybe I blink. Jostle the binoculars for no reason. Now it is a classic white boat of swanness, exquisite curve of its too-long neck regal, black bill held high. Royalty. No sign of muck-scooping.

I ask Uncle Dave various disjointed questions, faltering after each. *So . . . where did the squid come from? How big are they? What color? Have you seen them? Who found them? Does Silver Bay like having squid in it? Are they welcome there?* The conversation could be going anywhere. Just . . . why are there squid?

Uncle Dave doesn't make up answers. He only says what he sees, and even then, he doesn't go so far as to say everything's changing, but it is. Everything.

The photograph gives its clouds over to the warmth of low yellow light. But the sky behind already anticipates the pall of night. And the water reflects all of this upside down: the dashing yellow arrival, its sweep upon the bellies of the clouds. The firm, understated blue. And the blue's dignity, its eggshell perfection.

It is a photograph of twoness. Of reflection up and down, reflection left and right. It is a photograph of a doubled and doubling world.

Bill McKibben suggests with the title to his 2010 book that the planet we now live on is best understood as "Eaarth." Deeply familiar to inhabitants of Earth but profoundly—chemically— different. A close relative, an inexact double.

Of sea-sky chemistry, this is what I gather. During the past two hundred years of industrialization, the pH of surface ocean waters has fallen by 0.1 pH units. Because the pH scale, like the Richter scale, is logarithmic, this represents about a

30 percent increase in ocean acidity. And since 1970 carbon dioxide emissions have increased by roughly 90 percent; global carbon dioxide levels are now well over four hundred parts per million.

Chemistry aside, the mind can always set its anchor on the image of blunt volume. I recently learned Antarctica's ice sheet dumps 219 billion tons of ice into the ocean each year. That rate has tripled in the last decade.

The x-y axis brings back memories of calculus camp out at the Shrine of Saint Therese. High school juniors and seniors, big graphing calculators, a weekend's worth of camping gear. After lights out, in our rows of sleeping bags on the cabin floor, we sketched "kiss my asymptote" bumper stickers by headlamp.

In the museum photograph I see no asymptotes flattening their wings toward the distance of the margins, no parabolas curving up or down or any other way. Just that bold x-y axis.

Of penciling out calculus on reams of graph paper, I remember one last thing. You can set the x-y axis down arbitrarily. Anywhere on the paper. But once you do, it governs meaning across the whole grid.

The x-y axis also recalls a literary theory. Were we to chart this essay onto those same pale blue grids over which I pored as a teenager, we'd chart narrative along the x-axis, expressing actions and events as values of x. And we'd plot ideas vertically, expressing insights as values of y.

Therefore, if this museum photograph were a literary graph of events and ideas, we might say that the silhouetted shoreline *happens*, and that the kayak and contrail *think*.

Soon I'll go home and shower. I'll lay out my gear to dry for tomorrow. I'll listen to the marine weather forecast in the evening. I love that robot voice, how nonplussed he is in repeating *high of thirty-four* and *100 percent chance of rain* and *small vessel advisory* over and over and over, from Cross Sound down Chatham Strait, from Lynn Canal to Point Retreat, from Stephens Passage into Taku Inlet, mapping the archipelago on a loop. The marine weather forecast robot man is my lullaby, another uncle. He is reliable—even as he announces, between the lines, that nothing is as it was, that nothing is predictable, that a break in the pattern *is* the new normal.

Two vessels of transport mark the photograph's vertical axis. One preindustrial, one industrial. One human-powered, one reliant on fossil fuels. One designed to transport the lone individual; one designed for cargo, both human and non. One so close in the frame you can see the grain of the wood as textured and expressive as a face; one so far distant it isn't even visible. We see only its unmistakable trace in the sky.

Yet both transport. In this, they share common cause: both kayak and airplane derive from the impulse to journey, to depart, to go.

What's more, both kayak and airplane extend the scope of the world a human body can access. Both permit us to launch off the land into an aqueous medium, be it ocean or atmosphere. And I think there's something about shoving off from solid ground that many of us crave now and again. There's something out in the ebb and flow of fluid places we sense we'd do well to remember.

They go up Silver Bay on full moons, come back with squid. Salmon are eating them. Whales are eating them too. It's a new food source that's moved in, so it's good for everyone.

His tone, of course, is dark.

We understand this new nourishment as an unspooling.

The way we talk, some things get said and some go unspo-ken. In Utqiaġvik where another uncle lives—Uncle Geoff—some folks don't even use the phrase *climate change* any more. All seasons of the year are seven, eight, nine degrees warmer than they were when today's Elders were the agile youth, sup-porting the community with their hunting, their sewing, their building, their medicine. Uncle Geoff and his community are busy learning how to live on another planet. No, Utqiaġvik doesn't call it climate change; rather climate chang*ed*.

This is a photograph of precise division and balance. My day isn't making sense, but the photograph's mathematical control offers an antidote of orderliness. It is easy to look at. The eye travels horizontally. The eye travels vertically. Vision appre-ciates these simple seams, neat travel corridors up-down, down-up. Left-right, right-left. How easy, thinks the eye that has always loved algebra and the predictability of its x-y axis. How easy, thinks the eye, overlooking the composition's simil-itude to crosshairs.

I dreamed recently of a man made of ice. I knew him. Well. Seeing he'd come again—after such a long absence, after all we'd been through, and now made of ice—I grew furious. The metaphor struck me as trite. *Don't think you're showing me what you're made of*, I said, taking a stab at his gall. *You're only showing me what you think you know about yourself.* Later in the dream, I smashed his head.

Shattered ice flew across the carpet and now I wonder, had I observed more keenly, if that broken ice began to melt. I wonder if the shards grew glassy with a scrim of water, the idea of wet shuddering on every surface.

But at another point in the dream he was not made of ice and I had no fury. His presence was somehow free of context, our backstory gone in one clean rinse. I felt only the frictionless synchronicity with which we orbited a shared center of gravity, tracing and retracing one another's arcs in perfect revolutions. Physics, math, balance. Call it love.

Waking, I shuddered. Right then I felt my independence as a hard brace worn too long. The one made of ice, then, is perhaps not him at all. Yet it occurs to me it is not safe, in a warmed and warming world, to depend on what is frozen.

I go out Silver Bay but not to jig. To clamber up Bear Mountain with an old friend who grew up in Sitka, who's in Southeast because he's also visiting family for the holidays. What else can we do when it is clear and snowless? We hike up, up, up, steep, steep, steep, mostly trailless through forest holding to near-cliff. I learn the mountain formation across the bay is called Sugarloaf. The name is delicious and new in my mouth, though my friend assures me this is a common name for blocky-looking mountains everywhere. And I learn that down bay toward town is a mountain called Verstovia. To the right, one of the Sisters. Another Sister lies in the ambiguous beyond. As we climb, I keep saying I think I see her now, but my friend corrects me: no, she's not in sight, she's more *that* way.

We perch at the very top of a huge landslide where we have a line of sight on Mount Edgecumbe. It's an island volcano. A mountain topped with a crater rather than a peak. A classic form of volcanic geology, a classic form of Japanese painting. Plunked out in the ocean where it's easy to spot, form unmistakable so it can't be confused for anything it isn't, its symmetry a balm to the scattered mind.

And of course no balm at all, for it is a volcano, and no matter how many cherry blossoms the form evokes, a volcano remains a vent through which the earth explodes.

We dig our heels into the moss on Bear Mountain and face out toward Mount Edgecumbe in the distance. Looking afar permits us to rest by anchoring our balance, which wavers each time we dare glance down—straight down the landslide chute—at the wrinkled glaring skin of Silver Bay. Where young people jig for squid.

Has my friend heard of young people jigging for squid down there? Has he gone along with anyone, gone jigging for squid? It's very, very cold, and though we're not above tree line yet, it's breezy. We don't chat long before we need to move again.

In mathematics, the point at which the vertical axis and the horizontal axis cross one another is called the origin. Here, both x and y equal zero. In other words, the origin is the point from which an action is about to occur, the point from which an idea hovers, about to think.

These coastal mountains' literary tradition, oral, goes back to the beginning of time. It stems from the origin. Another way of saying it is that this place's literary tradition goes back to the time of glaciation, to the human migrations that followed the archipelago's slow birth out from under the ice sheet.

As a student of literature, I learned to differentiate between oral history, legend, and distant time. Oral histories depict relatively recent events. Personal narratives fit here. Legends recount a deeper history of transformation brought on by culture heroes. Reaching farther back even than legend are the distant time stories.

Reality was more malleable in distant time than it is now. For example, sometimes distant time orcas dive deep and walk around in human form where they live together in houses. Sometimes the mouse is a grandmother. Sometimes the glacier demands respect, and sometimes a human marries a bear. The rules of present reality aren't set in distant time the way they are now. The woman who marries a bear, for example, makes the best of it and has a family. Because things don't work out for them in the long term, the story marks a pivot point (one of many) in the world becoming as it now is: humans and bears no longer intermarry. But a complicated kinship persists.

The heart of what I learned is that as a body of literature, distant time stories trace the incremental transformation of a far-off, malleable reality into a fixed one. The one in which we presently live.

Or the one in which we used to live? I am thinking more and more often about that ancient malleability because it reminds me of the planetary flux of the present, the geochemical tumult of our seas and skies, how the established rules lose traction as deep patterns in the cycle of the seasons break underfoot, leave us walking on jostled fragments, glimpsing familiarity among the pieces.

I called the Sitka Fish and Game office recently. *What's with the squid?* I asked. Common market squid, I learned. Opalescents. No bag limits or possession limits in place because they're new. Regular sport fish permit will do. And people are indeed jigging for squid in Silver Bay, but don't forget they're also jigging down at the docks. The squid like the harbor lights.

The Sitka Sound Science Center also noticed the squid. Down at the Science Center, they know of a couple trollers keeping track of what they find in the bellies of caught salmon.

They also know of a troller who gives salmon stomach sacs to a university professor so *she* can keep track of what salmon are eating.

There's no disagreement, really. There never used to be squid around here; now there are. So it seems my uncle's basic gesture—watch what the young people are doing—is wise. We just don't know which among the old teachings will buoy us through life. And which practices we'll have to invent as we go, as the world's rhythms shift and tumble underfoot.

On the other side of the continent, they talk about a muskrat and a turtle. Back when the world was only ocean, when it was water from horizon to horizon. The world was watery like that for ages until one day the muskrat dove deep, scooped up a ball of mud, and the turtle offered her shell to bear the weight of it. Hence Turtle Island, as North America's been known since then, which gave us something to stand on. Something good and solid so that one day, over on this side of the continent, a raven could steal the sun, moon, and stars out of an old man's boxes and toss the first light up into the sky.

A muskrat scooped the mud. A turtle held it up. And a raven brought the light. History converged so that now, all of us land animals have something to blink about when squid come swimming up to the surface of Silver Bay on the full moon.

Anyway, out Harbor Point Road, it was no muskrat. It was a swan. A trumpeter. White feathered ass pointed to heaven, sturdy bill sifting underwater. Searching for just the right bottom muck to bring up into the day's blazing cold sun. We don't know yet what it's making, but we linger at the edge of its beach, gathering hints as best we can.

At some point in my middle childhood, I paddled alone from my family's protected campsite on the beach and headed toward the open water of Cross Sound. It takes no time for this fjordlands world to swallow us, for the human scale to fall through the cracks. And so no one watched child-me round the point into the glassy swell of open water for the simple reason that we were too small for one another to see.

I encountered a group of Steller sea lions riding that same powerful water. If I was in a trough, they'd already be riding up the wall of the next swell. I'd watch them as they rose, level with my boat, then level with my torso, then with the space above my head, suspended in the aqueous slope and breaking its surface to breathe their growly gravelly breaths and stare down at me. Then the passing swell would lower them and raise me to the top of the ambiguous fluid world where for a moment I could see the horizon, the trollers fishing miles out, nothing but the Gulf and the Pacific between any of us and Asia. Perhaps I was eleven. The experience made me, created me.

That is not altogether true. Before the experience, I was myself. After the experience, I was myself. So what I'll say instead is, perhaps everything in me cinched down. I became more set, shed a malleability I may or may not have really ever had. I remember thinking, *This is where I want to die.* Not an ominous idea at all, just a sensible touchstone I've carried into an unpredictable adulthood. *This is where I want to die.*

What pulled me around the point straight out to sea? And why did it mark me so?

Well, what child is ever *not* pulled outward and subsequently marked? Silent shifts in a person are the stuff of which we're made. It's a scoop of muck, if you will, lending early shape to something young and landless.

After that day in Cross Sound where alone in open water predators circled and did me no harm, after we all rode that swell turn upon turn, neither colliding nor capsizing, after I caught sight of that water's bodiless horizon over and over, after I tried and failed and tried and failed to memorize its farthest undulations, after I reached out and touched nothing— after that experience, I became more sure of the things that do not, as it turns out, have a center at all. Because I still remember a far rolling place where the earth simply isn't. Where no treetop scraggle stretches its ribbon of clean division between sea and sky. Where there is no unraveling double, no twin, no symmetrical repetition shaving its origin down to zero. Where there is just space for a beginning, and it never holds still.

NOTES

The photograph, titled *Blissed Out*, is the work of Naknek-based video and image maker Anna Hoover.

Bill McKibben's 2010 book is called *Eaarth: Making a Life on a Tough New Planet*.

A statistic is an artform. The ones appearing in this essay come from FiveThirtyEight's *Significant Digits* series, June 14, 2018; the National Oceanic and Atmospheric Administration; the Environmental Protection Agency; and ocean physicist Peter Wadhams's 2017 book, *A Farewell to Ice: A Report from the Arctic*.

OTTER MEDITATION

Someone cries out from the water. She thrusts her head and shoulders upward and lingers in the air for a still, silent moment, then peels off sideways. Her buoyancy fails and she slips beneath the sea. An eagle rides the air overhead. On the far side of the water, behind the small circles spreading and already dissipating in the silence, mist clings to a muscle of ice. The glacier is jagged and blue beneath an overlay of snow.

I am a small girl standing on the side of the road looking out over the water and clutching my father's index finger. He is concentrating. He wonders if he has understood. Someone is brokenhearted in the black and silver sea, and there is an eagle overhead. Across the cove, the curving tongue of glacier says nothing.

My coat is pink and I wear a muskrat fur hat. Since it is cold enough for me to wear fur, my father surely has his red anorak on, and perhaps his wool White Sox baseball cap. We come here often. Cars seldom drive on this road. It just borders the sea for a few miles at the north end of our island and peters out with a government-yellow sideways rectangle reading END ROAD. The sign is trimmed with a single black stripe.

Together, we do not stir until the cry reappears. We know it will. It does.

La voilà . . . I murmur. My grip tightens around my father's finger. We gaze at the woman's oily black head as her face pounds forward, throat cutting through the still water. She is a ways out but not distant enough to mask the exhaustion in each kick.

Though the exchange could not possibly happen in English, I'm sure my father points out to me it is not a seal. *Watch how she goes under*, he must say, for I am little and just learning how to read the shapes of animals in the water.

Yesterday the two of us took a sunny winter walk on this same stretch of the North Douglas Highway. Its uphill side is bordered by the steep ascension of rainforest. Sitka spruce and western hemlock stand together like so many Eiffel Towers—strong, silent, noticeably proud. Bald eagles sit high in these trees, yellow eyes flashing with every jerk of their heads. They scan the water and the rocky shoreline for prey.

Yesterday we saw a number of eagles, dark feathers fluffed against the winter chill. There are always eagles here because the cove is rich in marine life. But we remember one eagle in particular from yesterday's walk.

It was not the eagle's leap from high in the trees that stood out, although the weight of her body hurling off the thick branch hinted at a special urgency. And the moment of uncertainty as she plummeted for a split-second before her wings caught their confident hold on the air was terrifying, yes—but it was precisely in keeping with what one would expect if one kept constant company with eagles. And my father and I did. So we watched the raptor and nodded.

She rocketed out over the water and from our place onshore my father and I saw her pick once at the glassy surface. Success. Something big.

Comment ça? wondered my father. Prey that large is common during the summer gorging season, but the winter months here can be lean.

The eagle turned back toward shore, pumping her wings. The weight was too much. She landed in the snowy ditch up the road from us. I pushed my hat up my forehead so that wayward hairs of muskrat fur would not obstruct my view. My father craned his neck, his brow folding in on itself bit by bit. Neither of us could see into the sharp glint of snow over the edge of the road and into the ditch. I wiped my nose on a sleeve.

Soon the eagle had negotiated a better hold on her prey. She began pounding her wings again, gained purchase on the air, and lifted her dark load off the snow. Flying low and heavy she disappeared into the trees.

Traversons, said my father. This word always signaled great seriousness. My father and I took ritualized and unsmiling caution every time we crossed the road. I straightened my shoulders. We looked left. Then we looked right. No cars.

We crossed the road and walked along until we came to the place where the eagle had landed. Bright hot blood soaked the trampled snow. It was a lot of blood—but that was all. We went home.

Today, however, we have come back to the same place. But we face out toward the water, where a moaning, wailing, sometimes shrieking figure is passing back and forth, back and forth before this stretch of road. Her exhaustion is dreadful. I shiver in my pink coat and nudge closer to my father, pulling his index finger and drawing his hand in toward my face.

My father decides it was her baby the eagle fished out of the sea yesterday. He is pensive, stricken. Here is a mother in the sea, a mother without her baby, a mother who has searched for it all night. She is a sleek, dark, despairing river otter. Sleepless, she will cry here for five days before disappearing.

My father and I pick our way down the road in silence, turning to look out over the water each time the mother otter howls for her pup. My father is careful not to ask anything of me right away. It can be a wicked thing to disturb a child who is laboring with her thoughts. Still, he does not want me to lose myself in sorrow. He is responsible.

Tu sais . . . His voice trails off. He clears his throat. Then, softly, carefully—touched by my concentration? Fearing it, even? He creates a fragile image, one of two mothers. There is the mother otter and her pup in the sea, and there is the mother eagle and her eaglet in the nest. Both mothers would die for their babies. And both would murder the baby of another to feed their own. The hunting eagle is a good mother—or a good papa-mama, a term our family uses in both our languages, always intermingling meanings of fatherhood and mother-hood, merging the roles of nurturing and providing.

My jaw is tense. I hear him but blink half a dozen times and look at my boots, pressing the snow with a rounded toe.

Animals eat each other. They murder to feed their babies. As does my father, for me. Devotion, predation, blood, and love will become the pillars of an ongoing conversation. Thirty years later, the conversation continues.

The otter breaks the surface of the water again. She wails briefly. She swivels her head, peering over wet whiskers in the four cardinal directions, and gives another yelp before making a halfhearted dive. For a single moment her tail is flung up in the air, and it is only a small flop out in the water when she disappears. As I grow, learning to read dark shapes on the water, I will learn that this is the signature of the river otter.

This is distinct from a seal, whose head is round and looks like an orb bobbing in the water, and from a sea lion, whose head is triangular and looks sharp like a blade. A river otter is far smaller than either one, which suffices to distinguish otters at close range. But from afar, and because distance on the water is a trick to the eyes, one must always watch to see how the animal slips beneath the surface. For an otter, watch for a smooth curving dive, the small arc of which is followed by a tail momentarily flung skyward. The gesture is always an adieu, always a bon appétit, always a dark and sweet continuation. Watch very, very closely, for there will be no splash at all.

UPRIVER

TENDING TO BREAD

The cabin is shaped like an A because techs inhabit it for only two months of the year, and it has to stand up to the coastal Alaska storms pounding it for the other ten. The cabin's pointiness echoes the precipices and sharp summits surrounding it, but the mountains are not trimmed with red paint, and the cabin has no gargoyle of a glacier hunched on its shoulder. A river flows past, draining from a small lake where red salmon spawn to the tune of ice cracking on the mountain above. The reds are why techs come here, two or three miles up watershed from the sea of Prince William Sound, to summer over without electricity or plumbing or pavement or people. Gary and I are here for a season counting and killing fish in that river, listening to the ice overhead, and watching the rain fall.

The human genome for your gastrointestinal tract is as complex as for the rest of your body, Gary says. There is plenty of space for calmness to settle between his words, placing us on the peaceful side of his mood swings. *It's as unique as a fingerprint.*

Gary's back is turned because he is intent on scooting our diner-style spatula under a sourdough buckwheat cinnamon plantain pancake. He is at his calmest when he is cooking, and as his sole human companion during a summer of remote fieldwork, it is lucky for me when he can achieve tranquility.

The gastrointestinal tract is . . . Gary's words slow into silence for a moment. He has just gotten the spatula where he wants it. *A sort . . . of . . . center.* A sharp scoot, the jerk of the spatula, a turn of the wrist. He is unfazed by the thrill of a perfectly flipped pancake. *Digestion is a center of self.*

It is typical for the gastrointestinal tract to come up in casual conversation with Gary, but this morning is special. We are having a sourdough-inspired breakfast because I have decided I want to know how to use it in breadmaking.

Really? Gary had answered my announcement with a smile suddenly playing the edges of his mouth, eyebrows just noticeably livened. Nodding, he turned away.

But he had kept on nodding. This morning, then, pancakes: the universal celebratory breakfast.

Asking Gary to teach me something of his art has little to do with gaining a new skill. Once he saw a fish leap impossibly through—not over, and not beside, but through—a solid object protruding from the surface of the river. The description confounded me, and I asked questions that struck him as condescending, even patronizing. My knit brow had wounded him, although I did not understand this until later. At the time, it was all I could do to keep the camp running alone during the two full days Gary spent in silence, drafting long letters and staring at the spot where the fish had leapt.

The reality of our cohabitation in a two-person remote field camp involved flurries of such misunderstandings. Daily interaction demanded a pacifying force, a small structure to smooth the edges, to ground it in something basic.

Gary and I went to the same small liberal arts college, but our lives have intersected in one of Fish and Game's remote fish camps by accident. As students, we each had an acute awareness of the other; Gary's twin sister was my closest friend. He and she had the weight of history between them. They'd been linked since their time in the womb. But as best friends, she and I had the urgency of the present between us. For now, neither Gary nor I can usurp the place of the other in her life.

A memory: Gary, barefoot, in the sunlit halls of the philosophy building. We stand facing one another. After a time, he opens his backpack, hands me a grapefruit from inside, and continues down the hall. It is a wordless, straight-faced gift. The fruit has dimpled skin and I feel its round weight in my hand. Its waxiness and curvature consort with the sunlight in the hall as I turn it over. Then I slip off my shoes as well.

After graduation I go home to Alaska, and Gary turns his attention to the art of food. It is unexpected, then, that we should find ourselves standing side by side on the banks of the same river, left to our own devices to monitor this particular salmon run.

If I have a reason to seek out seasonal fieldwork, it is for the familiarity of remoteness in the coastal rainforest. If Gary has a reason, perhaps it is for adventure. Yet it is an adventure that pauses daily when he finds quiet in the kitchen, which I notice, first because it recalls the quiet I find in the out of doors and second because it marks a sharp contrast with the remainder of Gary's emotional spectrum.

I want to know how to make bread the way Gary does, not because I am interested in bread, but because I am interested in the way that food making softens the edge constantly sparring with Gary's peace of mind. Also, bread is basic. Fundamental. This appeals.

🌿

Either I am dreaming or not. The heavy, wet odor of cumin, fresh garlic, and cinnamon weighs like a sopping towel. With confusion at the moisture and an urge to vomit, I begin to wake. Pots bubble on the stove. It is the sound that registers first, a dim explanation of the sauna-like conditions turning my stomach upstairs in the loft.

A chopping sounds from the kitchen counter, directly below my pillow. But the nausea interrupts my will to investigate. Gary is restless. Hungry. Nighttime notwithstanding, his solution is to cook a four-course meal.

After the chopping comes grating, fresh nutmeg. And after the grating come six thwacks of a wooden spoon on the edge of the large cast iron pan. The oven door cranks open then slams shut. Metallic lids of various pots clatter. Gary swears. I shrink, contorted in my sleeping bag, myopic and dizzy with the shallowness of my breathing.

Eventually Gary turns off the heat. The bubbling in the pots subsides, but it is replaced by the eager sound of serving spoons. A final round of spiced steam clouds pours from each pot uncovered in turn.

Silverware clinks as he eats. The sound of his mastication is hypnotic. Then he heats water for the dishes. He washes them. He stacks them. He pours several gallons of rinse water down the drain, and I wish it was the river rising to sweep this red-trimmed A-frame with me in it out to sea.

When Gary returns to the loft and gets back into his sleeping bag, it is morning. His hunger has subsided, but I have come unglued. Gary sleeps. I do not. What is so nauseating about hot spiced steam? What is so painful about the confusion of waking to it? What would etiquette have dictated on his part, and what does it now dictate on mine? I feel blank. Does the real question lie elsewhere, in my sense of betrayal? Surely Gary's bout of nighttime cooking is a personal attack. Surely the havoc it wreaked on my sleep and my stomach not only proves but authenticates his hostility. Or does it reveal my own?

When he joins me downstairs later in the morning, I do not pitch a fit. Nor does he offer any excuse. His eyes leap about in their sockets. I want to ask him about the night. I want him to decode it, make sense of it, and laugh off my bewilderment, but the rug of reason has been pulled out from under our feet. The most I can hope for is solid footing, hard ground to stand on for the season.

🌿

Gary and I install the salmon weir in the river when we arrive in June. It stands like a metallic fence against the current, but by the end of the season will be almost irreparably warped by two months of constant water pressure. The purpose of the weir is to block spawning salmon from continuing upstream until we have counted them and let them pass. Three times we will keep the weir closed for several days, allowing the salmon run to build up like a fishy tidal wave so that we can trap several hundred and take the various measurements and tissue samples we contribute to the studies directed by biologists back at the office in town.

Every couple of weeks these same biologists send a float-plane to our camp. It brings us mail, grapefruit, yogurt, and M&Ms. It brings a naturopathic healing textbook for me, a local mushrooming guide for Gary, and the six kinds of unrefined flour we anticipate using in a series of collaborative breads. In exchange we send out scale samples collected with flat-tipped tweezers, otoliths (also tweezed) out from under the brains of sliced salmon skulls, and auxiliary fins collected with dog nail clippers and preserved in formaldehyde. It is the otolith take I like best. Otoliths are free-floating ear bones, each one roughly the size and shape of an oat of oatmeal, and because they grow in annual, concentric rings—like a tree—biologists can "read" otoliths to decipher clues about a salmon's past.

Our only real contact with the office occurs via satellite telephone every morning at nine thirty. We alternate calling in the counts—how many salmon we counted and passed through the weir yesterday and how many we blindly estimate might pass today—and the fisheries managers thank us profusely before consulting algorithms, spreadsheets, and other talismans unknown to us. They regulate the commercial fishing fleet accordingly.

Sourdough. Whole wheat flour, water, in a jar. Gary stands by our plywood table. Its white paint is peeling in some places. I sit on the three-legged stool under the window so that light, although smudged by the day's thick rain, can brighten the pages of my notebook.

He continues his dictation. *Cover it with a cloth. The consistency should be . . . like pancake batter.* Gary has taught classes on how to make kombucha, or fermented tea. Lesson time is serious. He expects me to take good notes.

I do. Check in sometimes and stir it up. Five or seven days until it gets sour? Then with each addition (more flour, more H_2O) it will decrease in sourness and later peak in two to four days. Smell it. Here I draw a Valentine because Gary is saying, *not just sniff sniff*—he holds his pinky up as if handling a porcelain teacup—*breathe it in. Smell it from the heart.* Gary, in all honesty, places his right hand on his chest. It is a solemn directive.

Then he drops his hand and shrugs. *If it looks funky, stir it in. But . . . if it looks really funky, pull out the funk.*

There is a pause. *Like mold.*

In a sense funk is the whole point of sourdough, but it must be kept in check. Gary raises his hands, cupping his fingers around the air to conjure the weight of a yeasty ideal. *When it reaches optimum sourness, add more flour and water to feed the yeast,* he says. Thoughts whistle through Gary's mind. He is deciding whether to make things more or less complicated for me. Finally he tilts his head. *That way the yeast won't start eating itself and get weird.*

🍃

Gary believes that a person's relationship with their fermenting foods is unique because living microorganisms need care. A person is responsible for preserving the welfare of their fermented foods over time—years, perhaps—and can develop an understanding of their live cultures' tastes and temperaments. *Fermented foods are ready when you are wanting to eat something now, and otherwise, they are a food to commune with. A mix between cooking and gardening,* he says.

The gardening comparison is apt because it emphasizes a truth about sourdough: it is alive. And as sixth grade outdoor survival classes insist, all living creatures need food, water, and shelter in one form or another. This is as true for the carrots and potatoes growing in your garden as it is for the culture of yeast growing in your sourdough.

The concept that living creatures have certain needs is taken up and directed at the dinner table in one of Gary's currently favorite books, *The Vegetarian Myth*. The author, Lierre Keith, raises the shrill question, "What will you feed your food?" She insists that all food is alive—it is either an animal, a plant, a fungus, a bacterium, and so on—and that before any of these can feed you, they themselves must eat, be nourished, and grow. In other words, first they must live, and then, in feeding you, they die.

The industrialized food system may obscure the fundamental connection between eating and killing, as well as between eating and living. But caring for one's food over time—whether in the form of raising chickens, cultivating wheat, or maintaining your own sourdough—can begin to make those fundamental connections clear again because it places the responsibility of care on the shoulders of the individual who will eventually kill the food he or she has nurtured, eat it, and be nourished.

🍃

I sit on the steps of our porch tying pieces of fish bones together with dental floss, making a mobile. Bits of salmon vertebrae, jawbones, and some dried gills lay in an open-air graveyard on the planks beside me. Gary comes out, sits down, and begins to read. We do not look at each other. Perhaps this is companionship. Is it a *National Geographic* in his hands?

Damn, he says. Then, *Brussels sprouts.*

I cradle a particularly toothy lower jawbone. I don't want to snap any of the teeth off of it trying to affix it to a piece of driftwood. But space for concentration was never guaranteed, no matter how far we are from town life. So I answer. *On the list, or finding out about them?*

They could be on the list. That's what I was finding out about them. He says this slowly, without lifting his eyes. Mutely, I nod. It is important, with Gary, not to say too much.

🌿

The ocean feeds the forest. Every summer, a seasonal silver wave of nutrients surges inland, both as basic and as essential as the pulse in your wrist. Here, it floods through major arteries and into myriad capillaries in the form of spawning salmon that course up rivers and into their tributaries. They carry the life force of the ocean. Salmon live for a handful of years in the dangerous luxury of the high sea where they absorb and become its wealth, then return to their natal streams where they spawn, die, and fuel a ritualistic frenzy of predatory gorging. The riches of their rotting carcasses are dispersed into the dense forests by sly overfed scavengers, high-flying eagles, and the fecal contributions of all. Fish yearly create this ecology of massive dripping trees and the impassably dense undergrowth, none of which could subsist on dirt alone. It is, after all, only a precariously thin layer of humus that overlays the bedrock of these mountainsides.

🌿

Out in the river wearing our GoreTex chest waders, rubber gloves, neoprene wrist guards, and nylon head nets, Gary and I pause in our salmon wrangling to discuss whether to push through to the end of the 540-fish sample that night or go in for dinner. We discuss the pros and cons of finishing. *Exhaustion is the only measurement I'm really going by,* says Gary.

The question causes Gary to recall something he read about a boy who had not yet learned to do anything other than push himself to exhaustion. The memory makes Gary laugh self-consciously. *I'm that boy!* It is one of the few exclamations he will make that summer.

Then he offers a counterpoint. *Not being exhausted is nice sometimes too,* he says. *That's one of the* abstract truths *I'm trying to come to terms with.* So we call it a day, gather our nets and knives, and start wading out of the river.

Gary climbs up the bank ahead of me and water pours from the folds in the fabric of his chest waders. He looks down at me from the bank. *Not being exhausted is nice sometimes too— it's actually more like one of the* esoteric principles *I'm still trying to come to terms with.*

The water is icy, the current unrelenting, and he is blocking my way out of the river. He is intent on finding the right words. So I listen, my legs numbing into posts against the water's steadfast rush. Whether self-restraint is an abstract truth or an esoteric principle, it is pushing to exhaustion that is natural for Gary. He is often riding the exhilarating edge of either physical or mental collapse. During the anorexia-laced years of his life, Gary subsisted on caffeine, air, and forceful human interaction. He says he was made for Wall Street. He may be right.

❧

Fingers are drumming this morning. There is a rhythmic thwack of fingerflesh on the plywood table. *Curried breads are really nice,* says Gary. He stares into my eyes. There is silence. The beginnings of ritual.

Squash, he says. His voice is soft, matched by the day's low flying raincloud.

Then quiet. Gary's face moves; his jaw scoots around and his eyebrows pull his forehead, testing the lay of the land.

Pumpkin seeds.

He gets up from the table to look at the spices. We tacked a colorful kitchen cloth onto the shelf above them. It hangs down like a curtain to shade the spice jars from sun that might weasel its way in through the kitchen window at odd hours of the nightless northern summer. When Gary lingers in front of the spice shelves, he has a habit of draping the cloth over his head and standing there like an old-fashioned photographer.

After a time, the words *maybe some nutmeg* make their way out from under the cloth's ketchup-colored trim. Then Gary ducks out from under the curtained spice shelf with his selection of small jars. His hands are nestlike. He holds the jars carefully, paternally.

🌿

You have two options when tweezing around in a salmon's cranial cavity. You can tweeze what you see or you can tweeze what you know.

First, there are the rules for getting in: one cut straight down at the back of the salmon's skull. A second cut perpendicular to the first, into its forehead above its eyes, shearing through the top half of its cream-colored brain. A slick triangular chunk of salmon head should detach neatly; flick it into the river. Now the options.

You can flip the bottom half of the lobotomized fish's brain up and out of the limpid dish where it floats and peer inside. You are looking for the otoliths, those free-floating oat-shaped ear bones. This may work with a king salmon, or a chum, or

65

a red. As long as the salmon is big enough its otoliths will be too, and you'll have a chance of spotting them in the mash of cranial fluids. Look attentively and tweeze what you see.

Your other option is to find the otoliths according to spatial prediction and your sense of touch. Use the memory of a thousand other otoliths, or the primordial resonance you feel with the body of the fish that feeds your landscape, that feeds your family. Your tweezers must be perfectly sensate: they are an extension not only of your fingers but of your humility. Slip the tip of the tweezers—open just enough to catch the hard, white bone you seek—under what is left of the salmon's brain. Do so at the right angle and your tweezers will meet each otolith just beneath and diagonally offset on either side of the brain. Swiftly tweeze what you know and trust.

Gary has steamed half a kabocha squash and pressed soft chunks of it into the bottom of our metal mixing bowl. Steam, thick and white like smoke, rises from the yellow mash. The windows are fogged over with steam escaping from the cook pot. It is rainy and windy and the cabin is cold enough for him to see his breath. Raingear drips pathetically by the door; it will not dry today.

Gary pours a bit of whole wheat flour into the bowl on top of the yellow squash. *Mostly it will be a spelt bread,* he says. *Because we have it.* He pours in some spelt flour. Then, some more. *About that much,* he tells me, not because there is any way to measure, but because I am the one who is learning and he is the one teaching me. Steam continues to curl up out of the bowl from the golden halo at the base of this soft wide cone of flour.

There is a shuffling sound as Gary shakes curry powder into the bowl. It lands dark and yellow on the pale molehill of flour.

It's not a spicy curry, murmurs Gary. And a moment later, *You can really smell the turmeric.*

The smell is thick, held by all of the steam in the room. He cooks with no ventilation when it is cold, when it feels like the glacier that oversees our work in the river has drawn our camp deep into its blue breast with one familial sweep.

Gary flips the jar up to read from its label: *coriander, turmeric, mustard, cumin, fenugreek, paprika, cayenne, cardamom, nutmeg, cinnamon, cloves.* He wants a spicier bread, though, and adds more cayenne. Three solid thwacks to the base of the jar by the heel of the hand. The deep tomato-colored chili powder on top of the saffron yellow of curry and turmeric is beautiful. They are rich, warm colors, bright, and recall a favorite wildflower of mine, the orange-petaled, yellow-spurred columbine whose face turns downward in a perpetual posture of grief. The colors are out of step with the palette surrounding us. Grays, silvers, and whites vie only with greens here—sky, clouds, rain, fog, sea, ice, and the verdant bursting of coastal Alaska's old-growth rainforest.

Gary sprinkles dried cranberries into the mix. Stirs. Raw ingredients turn to dough. He hollows a pit in the dough and half spoons, half pours the sourdough into it like gravy as one would in one's mashed potatoes. Stirs again. Adds some water. *About . . . that much,* he says for my benefit.

Gary wraps a kitchen cloth around the mixing bowl, heavy with the sticky mass of bread dough in it. We leave the bread to rise. Gary turns to feed the sourdough, pouring an even stream of whole wheat flour into the jar. When flour spills on my forearm it feels surprisingly soft. *Oops,* whispers Gary.

67

🌿

To break bread with thine enemies. Give seed to the sower, and bread to the eater. Give us this day our daily bread.

The staff of life.

Bread: Biblically basic. Sanctified sustenance.

Killing food by eating it: The most essential act of living.

Sourdough: Cyclic. Dynamic. Growth, death, absorption, evolution. Feeding your food, sustaining your sustenance; tending *to*, caring *for*.

🌿

Our squash curry bread dough goes into the oven a day later. Gary says we let it sit too long. It sounds like damage. But Gary is calm, determined to move slowly, speak softly, and feed himself.

He sprinkles some flour into the bottom of a large pan. This loaf will bake in free form, sitting as a roundish blob of dough on a flat surface. Gary begins to ease the dough out of the mixing bowl, careful not to break the internal structure built by the sourdough's feasting yeasts.

It is a strikingly yellow dough. Not a beaming dandelion bright, but yellow with a little darkness, a little depth. It reminds me of a brick: heavy colored with a rough texture. But while the color itself is dense and strong and the texture is stubbornly sticky and earthen, the mixture has a fragility inherent in the fact of its being alive. Gary's hands know both of these truths.

He is utterly engrossed in this act of care. He has a history with these microorganisms. He started the sourdough when we first arrived at this camp; has checked on it daily since then; fed, watered, and stirred it; and every so often used the sourdough in his baking. But what intrigues me is that somewhere in the arc of this ongoing relationship, Gary's caring for his food morphs into a sort of caring for himself. He is pulled toward an urgent pace but seeks to live slowly, gently, and perhaps it is that tension that leaves a thin spot in his composure, easily pierced like bubblegum stretched to translucence. It is not the forcefully quiet demeanor he cultivates that evens his keel, but rather the ongoing practice of feeding his food, of nurturing the ingredients he will later use to feed himself. After taking the bread out of the oven, Gary gazes at it on the counter, lightly tapping its domed crust. He cuts the first slice cleanly. Steam pours from inside the loaf, and I wonder if the best way to care for the human heart is to spill that same heart into the care of something else.

CONFETTI

Their ears are large
Their feet are small
They haven't any chins at all.
But I think mice
Are rather nice.
    —Unknown children's book

*M*arion's fingers are a little bit longer than war-
ranted by such a slight body and her joints
point sharply. The effect is elfin. And rather
like mice, she doesn't have any chin to speak of.

What was the most beautiful part of your day? she will ask
me, beaming, delighting in my hesitation, my uncertainty.
When I can't think of what to say, I resort to deflection. I turn
the question back to Marion, and she will give an immediate
answer. The moment a crisp banjo string snapped under her
fingers, perhaps, or the ravens' chaotic involvement in her
afternoon at the dump, or better yet, the cold pepperoni pizza
a lady in green covertly shared with her upstairs in the book-
store. When all I do is blink Marion will throw the thinnest
arms around my neck, calling me a*dork*able and nuzzling her

way into a snuggle from which I won't be able to disentangle either my limbs or my once-independent mind.

Much like a stick figure pressing onward through the squares of a cartoon, Marion walks bent too far forward at the waist. She must be nursing some protracted ailment of the lungs—perhaps her ribs are too fragile to properly house the meager collection of vital organs impossibly lodged inside her paper-thinness. Should she ever straighten her shoulders and throw back her head, one can only assume her skeleton would snap dryly to pieces like uncooked spaghetti noodles. But the image may be unnecessary. Recent periods of adolescent homelessness and indigence all but confirm my hunch that Marion suffers from some unmitigated pulmonary disorder that causes her to bend unthinking from the waist even as she springs from this side of the parking lot to that and back again.

But sympathy here confuses the experience at hand. When my worries go toward lung disease songbirds leapfrog in waves overhead, dizzying my eyes' skyward glance as Marion, tugging my wrist, brightly welcomes me to the old green van. This is her new home, a whimsically decorated broken-down shell of a vehicle with a drooping mattress in back—the very first private space she has called her own. Its seats have long since been removed and the plywood floor is well-swept but there is no denying the accumulated cigarette butts lining the cracks between wood and van wall, nor the single camp pot encrusted with the remnants of some weeks-old meal given to her by a bewildered new friend taken by the notion that someone as "full of life" as Marion ought to eat something—anything—her skeletal thinness is, after all, so eerie.

Marion doesn't think to give the pot back. She hasn't anything to cook in it and no thought of acquiring anything to cook anyway. It never occurs to her that the pot's original owner might have a habit of cooking and eating food her-self, daily even, and so might miss it. Marion imagines many beautiful things like cavorting unicorns and tambourine-play-ing owls and knit caps the color of streaming sunshine, all of which translate into the trancelike guitar solos those long loose fingers of hers unhinge from any stray instrument she gets ahold of. But she does not imagine such things as other people's habits.

Nor does she imagine that a winter nighttime walk across town will beat the buoyancy of her mood. But it does. I will soon be driving Marion out to a bar to cheer her up. When she realizes she may lose a couple of her toes to frostbite, this is her request.

This is her request because last night she was sitting on someone's kitchen counter listlessly flopping the phone cord back and forth. *Pain? Yeah, hurts pretty bad,* she had said into the phone. Then, *Can't tell. My fingers might still be too numb. . . . No, yeah, I'll use a fork. . . . Okay, let's say yes I can feel my toes and yes it's painful.*

The nurse on the other end of the line must have asked what color they were because Marion had shouted *Red!* as if a right answer delivered at top volume had the potential to win her a prize. A sticky one, probably, of the sort discovered in the bottom of a box of Cracker Jacks.

Well, as long as her toes aren't gray—

Um . . . define gray, Marion had said. *I mean I guess yes. So ten gray ones.* Well, as long as she hasn't been rubbing them—

I wasn't supposed to rub them? This one had genuinely piqued her curiosity.

Well, as long as there aren't any blisters—

I'd say I have quite a few blisters, shall I count?

Well, as long as she leaves them alone and lets them pop naturally—

Okay, but a few of them popped while I was rubbing them just now.

There had been a scramble on the other end of the line and stern talk of infection. Marion thanked the nurse, accepted a small stash of someone's dog's leftover antibiotics, wandered out of the kitchen, and eventually left the apartment. No one was really sure afterward whether they ought to have helped her home.

The next morning she ate chocolate ice cream for breakfast in her van and now she wants to go out and because I am confounded not only by the combination of potential amputation and chocolate ice cream but even more so by my recollection that Marion looked so whitish and limp on that kitchen counter, I will not drive her to a health clinic at all, because she doesn't feel like it, but to a bar, because she does.

Although I am driving I still see the sharp edge of the kitchen counter cutting into her soft thighs. I glance like the responsible driver I am from the double yellow line between lanes to the single white one but I mostly just see her spindly legs dangling in the air. It occurs to me that perhaps her feet never consorted much with the earth in the first place, that Marion does more floating than anything else, that she should see a doctor, that I don't really like this bar we're going to, that my stomach is still sour from its sudden start at the sight of those limp legs hanging off the edge of the kitchen counter, legs that just buckled beneath her when Marion tried to launch herself into the air after hanging up the phone. These are the things that will occur to me but the things I know to be reasonable sometimes lose their shape in my dealings with Marion and I will find I have no hesitation to do what she so sweetly and incomprehensibly wishes.

As I drive, Marion suddenly thrills at the opportunity to play a Patsy Cline cassette on her battery-operated tape deck.

For some reason neither of us turn off the car radio. The Subaru is filled with two musics at once, discordant, disjointed sound qualities clashing from the mismatch of the car's speakers and those of the tape deck. Maybe Marion and I are also trying to talk to each other over Patsy and the radio and maybe not. Eventually, when for sure there is nothing, really, to say, Marion just holds my gaze with her gleeful silent smile. She is pressing me into a most distant sense of solitude.

It is fitting, then, that I am reduced to a clinging giggling mess as, arm in arm, Marion and I fuse into a single flailing wool-clad creature attempting to gain purchase on the ice-slicked incline leading to the bar's front steps. After a minute this becomes maddening—if only that bottom step were within reach—but the innocent thwarting of simple intentions is met with as much apology as one can expect of a confetti-filled firecracker and the night leaves me to my own devices.

When we do make it inside the smoke-filled barroom Marion and I step apart. She is comfortable here. But I feel kind of like an unhitched trailer, reliant upon the motor power of another vehicle and inconvenient to tow in a crosswind. Still, I am here, and so I shed one or two outer layers to keep busy. Meaning to disguise my squeamishness about wool's absorption of cigarette smoke, I toss a sweater here and a scarf there with false insouciance. Marion has already limped over to the wicker chairs in back. Nearby, someone's guitar case sits open and empty on the floor. Yellow flames leap from the grill where squealing women are flipping burgers. Someone's dog is wandering from barstool to barstool, less interested in snarfing bar snacks than in sampling crotch odors. The surprising number of empty beer pitchers sitting on all of the room's available surfaces suggests that no one is particularly concerned with busing the tables tonight. The talk is gruff

and accusatory and careless. Marion—head bowed and rock-
ing, eyes closed, mouth expressionless, and neck crooked at a
heart-wrenching angle recalling the rigor mortis of a broken
bird—plays someone's guitar.

That is when the absence of a chin strikes me not as
comely or cute but as tragic. Marion plays with the enormity
of a heart that intends to spend itself hard and fast. And her
chin that isn't there has left its space to the impossible crook
of her spine. From the front all I see is the rolling crown of her
head and the bony ice-colored nape of her neck in the light of
the bar's neon beer signs. But her fingers are prideful of their
long slenderness and eager to be gazed at. They move to be
seen. They do.

Like this Marion plays folk music with a flair of the
Baroque. It is not stylistic in its formality, but in its water-like
repetitions, its tumbling variations, its allegiance to a theme.
She is bent and broken and entranced over an acoustic guitar
that I know is filled simply with air but which appears truly to
be her only anchor to these floorboards. The planks underfoot groan with the weight of everyone else's lurching steps,
yet as she plays, Marion's physicality blends with the notes as
a vapor. The music is at once flighty and fleeting yet persistent.
It is made of an otherworldly plucking that pours out as if from
a mass warbling contingent of chickadees.

The branches off of which such tiny birds flit can be as
thin and slight as sticks of incense. On cue, the smoke in the
bar takes on the dry scent of jasmine and ginger. I linger, dis-
oriented, holding a couple of two-dollar mystery beers and
unsure of where to set them. Marion is perched in a tree, her
toes unfrozen and strong and curled around a high branch's
skyward twigs. Of course she is still embracing a guitar. Of
course her thin neck still bends impossibly, all but broken

76

before the force of her fingers' abandon. From the ground I hear not the notes but their form, the pattern stated and restated so quickly and seamlessly as to achieve a chant-like lull, broken only with a most disconcerting chord change that does not touch the spilling pattern of sound but changes it unalterably, like light shifting over the bustling army of tiny birds whose winter lives I can't quite fathom.

AT SEA

THE FUNERAL

BY PLANE, PART ONE

My seatmate is in her seventies with a solid frame and a mannish nose, and we will share a death but not our names. She wears a big khaki-colored jacket full of cargo pockets in which she rummages first to check on her half-spent cigarette, later for a damp tissue. Wrappers come out, go back in without inspection. *Betcha this pen is dead,* she crows, transferring a chewed ballpoint from somewhere in a breast pocket to a Velcro flap by her thigh. I may have seen hands like this before but can't place them. Something I say about the chewed pen delights her so her eyes scrunch closed and the bridge of her mannish nose scrunches too and she purses her lips so that only her two front teeth show in this thing of a smile. Leaning left and right in a couple of quick sways she finger-fans her face and chortles. It is a gravelly cooing.

She addresses anyone who lingers in the aisle, anyone who looks like they might be assigned the center seat in our row, calling out, *Are you nice? We like 'em nice*—and thunking my arm with the back of her hand—*We like 'em nice, don't we.* Yes, we do. But we also agree that the value of nice airplane seatmates is surpassed by the absence of said seatmates. We

81

high-five over the point. Plane rides to Alaska can be giddy and self-congratulatory like this. Particularly in December.

I've called her mannish, but then there's her tawny hair, thin and full of air so that it doesn't much hide the skin of her skull. It's a nearly troubling trace of femininity, for it is, despite itself, revealing. At least she is free of the handbag—this is a woman who didn't bring a purse. Or anything else. She doesn't need anything to *do* during the flight. She will sleep under her jacket's cavernous hood, because she won't have bothered to take off her jacket on the plane. She won't bother taking off her jacket now, and later, she won't bother to zip it shut, even though four days of steady snow will shift to freezing rain within minutes of our flight's touchdown. She hasn't any idea which pocket holds her wallet and which holds her cigarettes, but I figure she has the old habit of finding what she needs by patting herself from the breasts down, both hands at a time.

They're too long, these hands. And dry, too dry. Skin that's tight, brittle, susceptible to tearing, like a discarded paper bag, and stained with uneven freckled blotches. Hands with intelligence, though. Hands that have worked, that are competent, that may commit sly acts in and among those pockets with or without this woman's intent. *Four kids*, she says now and again, leaning in to conspire about this or that and snapping back to falsely innocent attention when a flight attendant squeezes past. She says she is always getting in trouble with those people; I riff on airplane authority, and she roars. Later, she will pull that khaki-colored hood over her head, tug the strings on either side, and snore inside its cave, a cave from which only her strong hooked nose protrudes. Things are well in hand. She'll wake up in Alaska and someone else will heft her checked bags, overstuffed with what-all for the grandkids, into the trunk of her daughter's Subaru.

I don't actually know what kind of car her daughter drives. But we are flying to Alaska, so I do know what kind of car her daughter drives. Her daughter drives a Subaru.

BY FERRY, PART ONE

A eurohawk is not a straight mohawk. No, hairstylists classify a eurohawk as *a fauxhawk variant.* It involves longer hair down the center of the head and shorter hair on the sides. I now know this because I will tell someone about the little girl on the ferry growing out her mohawk and will be corrected: it sounds more like a eurohawk.

But at the moment she's unclassified, a spiny and feral seven-year-old evading supervision and putting her hands over her ears. Patting them slowly, then faster. Opened, closed, open, close. Opencloseopencloseopen. I remember doing this when my mother ran the vacuum, so I mimic the girl. We don't smile across the deck of the ferry, but we watch each other and pat our ears, listening to the alternate muffling and roaring of the boat engines. When this girl runs over to me it's to shout that she can make the sound of a duck. She cups her hands over her mouth, and I have to lean in close to hear the duck over the engines of the ferry. We're out on the deck under the solarium contending with the drone of diesel, the drone of wind, and the drone of ripped water getting split into those twin waves that peel away off the hull. Our faces are pink from cold and salt. We like it out here. When she makes a duck sound, I see she has one missing front tooth and one grown-up tooth coming in.

A grandmother with dangly earrings and a new polar fleece is here to interrupt. The fleece is insufficient for her summer trip to Alaska, I gather, because she walks tight and hunched against the air. New fleece says to the girl *are you bothering people again* and I will her away, ask the girl what kind of duck. *A mallard*, she answers, apologizing that she doesn't know if she's doing it right. But a mallard.

The grandmother is visiting from Michigan. Her son teaches school in Sitka and he and his wife are raising their daughter there, so the grandmother comes to Alaska to visit family. She took her granddaughter to Juneau for the weekend and they're ferrying home to Sitka today. Is that where I'm going? Yes, this ferry also stops in the Native village of Angoon, but I, like the grandmother, am going to Sitka. She thinks Sitka's so pretty, don't I? Of course I do. And so is Juneau, but Sitka's just unbeatable. Of course it is. But she could never live there, could I? Because her no, not with bears all the time and rain all the time and dark winters and only however many stoplights—do I know how many stoplights there are in Sitka?— well, believe her, it's a lot less than Lansing and she likes bears plenty, just not so all the time as in Sitka.

Juneau, population: 30,000. Mostly on the mainland. At the mouth of Lynn Canal, north of Taku Inlet. Eleven percent Native. Sixty miles from Angoon.

Angoon, population: 450. A Tlingit village on Admiralty Island at the mouth of Kootznahoo Inlet, off of Chatham Strait. Eighty-two percent Native. Forty miles from Sitka.

Sitka, population: 9,000. On the outer coast of Baranof Island. Twenty-five percent Native. Not particularly shielded from the Gulf of Alaska by Kruzof Island's 3,200-foot dormant volcano, Mount Edgecumbe.

BY FERRY. PART TWO

It's the kids who come and go from the solarium during those early minutes leaving port. The solarium is outside, up top, and at the back of the ferry. It's kind of a three-sided green-house with scratched, warped plastic paneling on the sides and roof that shields a section of the deck from rain and sleet. There is no fourth wall; the ferry's back deck extends out from the solarium. Everyone wants to sit indoors out of the weather but no one can get their kids to stay still so they go indoors, outdoors, upstairs, downstairs. They're excited. Discovering the ferry, learning the layout of the cafeteria and the lounge, and finding out how forcefully toilets flush on a boat.

A little later, when the kids are bored to pieces or plugged in to electronics, there is a lull in traffic to the solarium. No one out there but me.

The marine highway has a bothersome aesthetic policy, which is that all of our ferries have an American flag attached to the back, a flag that whips around with violence in the wind of sea travel. If you're going to sit outside in the solarium and bundle up, or nestle in your sleeping bag on a plastic lawn chair under the heat lamps, you end up planted at roughly eye level with the American flag attached to the back of the boat. It is red and white and blue and flinging around between you and everything you might care to look at, slapping itself over and over and over. Hours of ferry travel are good for check-ing out avalanche chutes and ridgeline cornices or scanning the water for wildlife, fishing boats, driftwood, anything. But somehow my eyes always settle back on the snaking red and white stripes. I find myself fixed and staring, mind lulled into something mushier than is pleasant, and the next time, a bit mushier still.

It's early in the ferry ride, though, so I'm not alone for long because the kids' antsiness transfers two generations up and now retirees need to stretch their legs. They filter outside onto the deck, bending their knees, zipping the neck of new coats, fussing with the wrist bands of their gloves. It's gorgeous out here but they're chilled, have been all week, probably will be until the connecting flight they catch in Seattle delivers them back to the tarmac of whatever city's July they've traded in for a glimpse of the north.

Once we're hours into the ride, with hours more to go, anyone could be drifting out into the solarium. Professionals of various stripes come out for a smoke. *God, it's beautiful—the mountains—oh, look! Look out at that, look over here, look at whatever I'm looking at so that we're both looking at it.* An adjusted purse strap, a flick of the ash. Full disclosure: in this paragraph there's no telling the tourists from the locals. Adults in general are uniformly exclamatory about the view and fixated on directing the attention of others.

The tap dancers, however, are different. I place them in their mid-fifties. They wear sunglasses, down vests, and midleg zip-off hiking pants in earthy hues. Quick-drying and paired with reasonably sidewalk-worn sneakers. He has a peppered white beard; she has dark loose curls. They come out to the solarium and tap side by side, then him in front and her behind. They're quite good. And then they look a bit at the sun on the sea and the snow on the mountains and go back in. Both pairs of hands remain pocketed throughout.

THE FUNERAL

The way to coax them into letting you step off the ferry when it pauses in Angoon is to skip the purser's desk and go straight down to the car deck. Look for someone in a fluorescent yellow vest because the people in fluorescent yellow know how things work. They know which ferry terminals have empty vending machines, what the current Maritime Security level is, and who at each port is and isn't going to hassle loitering backpackers when MARSEC is on orange. Because they manage the car deck, they also know everything about their passengers: whose dog, alone for hours, has been barking all day in the belly of the boat; who walked on with a kayak and will need a hand hauling it up the ramp; who was forced to park too close to a gigantic rented RV and will have to crawl across the passenger's seat to start their own vehicle; whose gas container or rifle is locked in the car deck gun case; and who's wandered off the ferry and needs to wander back on before the next sailing gets underway. The people in fluorescent yellow are not authoritarian and are not in charge. They are simply indispensable.

We dock in Angoon and the fluorescent I accost has a face so young that her squash-colored ponytail seems both holy and babyish. It's hair reminiscent of the silver fuzz marking certain newborns as angelic and ghostly, newborn fuzz that hums with its own glow, that still sends a shiver down a mother's spine long after it has faded into something normal and mammalian. When I ask her if I have time to get off the ferry for a few minutes, she turns and her huge yellow vest pushes against my whole side body because she's leaned in to add discretion to the news: *They're having a funeral!* Her body is soft and I think to step back, but don't, and answer her pressure with my own. Her body is soft and they are having a funeral and because we are pressed against one another and my question is unanswered, we make small talk. I learn that yes, the body is getting buried here in Angoon, and no, the death didn't happen in Juneau, the body was only sent there to be embalmed, and did I know what she means, because she doesn't think they do that here, but maybe if I just walk off the ferry up the ramp I can ask Carey in the parking lot how long we have in port.

She turns away and there is a new and immediate chill where our torsos have separated, lighting an odd sadness in the place where her warmth has vanished. The temperature of the absence is heavier, somehow, than was the weight of being pressed against her.

At the top of the ramp, Carey has a fluorescent vest too, but it's orange. He squints and is shaved more cleanly than necessary. Is it okay if I get off the ferry, walk around some? *There's a funeral,* he answers. I nod and so does he. I ask my question again. A sigh. *You probably have a few minutes.* Five? I ask him. Or twenty-five? Or, probably less? He signals the pickup at the base of the ramp and says to me that there's not really anywhere to go. My silent retort is that there's nowhere *not* to go. Pretty great beach over there, I answer. Carey glances. *Never been.* It's a good beach. Do you think fifteen minutes. *Well. We won't leave without you,* he says, and I step off the ramp into the ferry terminal parking lot. It's an okay gravel pad a couple miles outside the village.

I've bivy-sacked in this parking lot in years past, and each time a 3:00 a.m. ferry drop-off left me stranded with camping gear I couldn't pack until daybreak. I've launched my kayak a number of times from this spot. But now it's midday and everything is easy when a girl gets herself off the false flatness of a parking lot and onto the rocky mellow incline between sea and mountainside. There are these rocks down there, layered, moguls of exposed bedrock, but colored like the belly of a clam or like the cream-green interior of a shell. I don't know why all the other rocks in this archipelago seem to be blue-gray shales, but they are, and these aren't. It's their sweepy layers that make them look all the more like shells, massive ones. Bedrock made of curls may well be set down by the mollusk of the earth, calcium deposit by calcium deposit, to cage its own translucent underbelly somewhere under the sea.

But I don't walk far and when I'm back in sight of the ferry, the gravel pad has become choked with vehicles and a crowd. The ferry can't load and depart; a green pickup truck with the body in back has stopped twenty yards off the ramp and everyone has gathered. The parking lot is filled with a crowd that can't be parted to load the ferry because someone's talking. Slowly.

The funeral has started early; we are having it in the parking lot. The mood isn't dark, but there's an older gal in a purple fleece in charge of weeping, leaning alternately on various folks' arms, then steadying herself with the tops of children's heads. Young Native moms press toddlers to their hips or stand tilting forward, leaning on strollers. Many wear sweatpants. Young Native dads mill around in baggy jeans sort of watching one child or another, responsibility shifting child to child as little ones bustle freely around the parking lot. Adolescents pod up, giggle, make no sound. No one, in fact, makes any sound because an Elder is speaking over the body. My ears catch only stray consonants, too few to follow. He's by the truck and I can't hear him, can't even tell when he's gone back into English from the Tlingit. Should I strain to hear? Are others straining? It doesn't seem so. The crowd is totally respectful, silent, but not paying attention.

People enjoy gathering. There's been a loss, but they like it that they have assembled in the ferry terminal parking lot, that everyone's out in the same place. An eagle flies low over the little crowd, peering into it, and most people don't look up but two men behind me watch the raptor and agree in slow whispers that he's been watching and considers it to be over now, finished.

It? What is it? Does the eagle see a resolution in the funeral before any of the people do, before they rouse themselves for

dispersal? What is it that's over for the eagle when the people don't budge under the inaudible words of the Elder? The
Elder is inspired but he is also frail. He seems almost to nod
off while speaking and keeps one hand on the side of the green
pickup truck partly in a posture of authority and partly to stay
awake. I think of my own grandfather, how his eyelids would
close, sometimes mid-sentence. I think of the eagle, flying low,
a silent sense of conclusion closing in behind his glide. What
is it that the eagle already knows?

Eternity comes and goes and six blue-jeaned guys climb
into the back of the green pickup. They sit three to a side in the
bed of the truck, the body between them in what appears to be
a black plastic fish box. Cardboard sheets are strapped to its
sides. A button blanket and a wooden carving lie on top. The
blanket, a glorious primary blue rimmed with primary red, is
totemically patterned with spaced white buttons. I can't get a
clear view of the button blanket, but the carving looks like a
wolf. None of this is arranged to disguise the black plastic and
the cardboard; even from a distance it looks like a big fish box
in back but it's not, it's a body, and she was a lot of people's
great-grandmother. She has come from Juneau in a plastic box
with cardboard sheets strapped to the sides and tribal regalia
sitting on top. Followed by another pickup truck packed with
store-bought bouquets, she has been met at the ferry terminal
by a couple hundred people. Headed into the dark seaside forest the flower truck will follow the fish-boxed body with a load
of tiger lilies. Its bed is full of five-gallon buckets packed with
cellophaned bunches of them.

No one is shushing the weeper in purple polar fleece, no
one is rude to the Elder who may or may not be blessing the
body in the parking lot, and no one is distressed by the child
in gray who has been marching about with a diaper leak. The

large wet region on the front of its little gray sweat suit spreads. It can wait.

In another life, the ferry is back underway and it's only a cupful of hours to Sitka. I pass the time copying passages from Anne Carson's "The Glass Essay." Example: "You remember too much, my mother said to me recently. Why hold on to all that? And I said, where can I put it down? She shifted to a question about airports."

BY PLANE, PART TWO

Even on the plane to Alaska, where you always know someone and feel good greeting them, where you accidentally make new friends and arrive somehow bonded to everyone else who went north that day—even on such a flight, travel is evasion. It's cutting loose, not looking back. There's a jostle of connection, of banding together, but like all travel there's schism folded in and lone secrecy at the core.

The woman in her cargo-pocketed jacket is flying to Juneau for solstice and ferrying to Angoon for Christmas and what about me. But the word *Angoon* blooms this ferry-halting parking lot funeral into my mind and now I am telling her about it for I must return to the funeral out loud, to the parking lot with the state ferry stuck, unable to load, while the villagers have a speech they can't hear. She is in her cargo pocket jacket, and I am twisting toward her under my seatbelt, poking a good sturdy stick of memory into the campfire between us. We're two travelers leaning into the same orange heat, and I say something of my fondness for Angoon. I say once there was a funeral, and I say the ferry just waited, and already she has clapped those blotched, dry hands. She has clapped them and crows to me about the truck of cellophaned lilies, and I say yes, I say yes was she really there, I say yes and does she remember the weeper in purple polar fleece and *she* says yes, howls it nearly, volleying back about the eagle's dismissal, do I remember its sweet low glide over the crowd? We tumble like this on last summer's ferry, the campfire between us throwing sparks that zip up and out, trails bright and fast and always gone, traceless paths already lost as they are lit.

CHENEGA

Home is always border country.
—J. Edward Chamberlin, *If This Is Your Land,*
Where Are Your Stories?

he coastal rainforest of North America is an organism. On Good Friday 1964, it shudders at its northern crest and a 9.2-magnitude earthquake lurches entire islands. Underwater landslides send the sea slamming as tsunamis into mountainsides.

The island of Chenega, for example, ends up fifty-two feet to the south. And a wave wipes the village of Chenega off the island.

Now it is an island without a village, fifty-two feet less north.

There is still, however, the schoolhouse. On a knoll ninety feet above tideline, its remnants lean into the same rain and wind that have always stirred this dark forest, swept this chill air.

I remember that schoolhouse. The silvered wood that's left of it. I remember curving along the arc of Chenega Bay in 2008, half fish, wearing my kayak as I wear my body. Wearing both last summer as I wear both now, playing out my part, as does each barnacle, each summer squall, each sea lion, rockfish, and murrelet, each spawning salmon returning from its years at sea, each drop of the relentless rain, each layer of slate and shale.

Yes, I wear my boat as I wear my body, but its material is not animal-soft like the rest of me. The boat is made of glass. Fiberglass and Kevlar composite, painted a mellow sherbet orange. I wear it as I wear my body but also as something *other*, the way I wear these peeling curls of dead skin, yellow, hardened with rigor mortis, refusing to slough off.

On maps, the coastal forest organism is shaped like a seahorse, tip of the tail fanning so far south as to reach into California. Its trees thicken through Washington, lungs full along the coast of British Columbia, ribby side body stretched taut through the lengthening winters of Southeast Alaska. Then the organism curves in a yawn all the way over and above the Gulf. In the crook of that northernmost curl of the rainforest is Prince William Sound, where fjords show up as sinews of sea wrapping the base of forested mountains.

The shape of the continent's northwest coastal rainforest isn't, as Melville would say, down on most maps.

But rest assured. It is a single organism. Whether I am summering beach-to-beach in one part or in another, summers on the water form a clean continuity. The thousand rippling miles of cool, dark coast live according to a long, slow heartbeat, one I myself will live and die too quickly to discern. I hold the conviction that less than a single pulse of that heartbeat will have propelled me through this life.

Disaster echoes here in quarter-century intervals. Following the Good Friday earthquake of 1964 is the Good Friday *Exxon Valdez* oil spill of 1989. I was a child during the latter.

The lore of 1964, year of the quake: Elders and old-timers recall it. Parts of Anchorage broke, crumbled, and were rebuilt.

And on Kodiak Island, the village of Old Harbor saw three waves. There were two that simply splashed a few homes, then a third that washed most of the village out to sea. The school and church remained intact, and so Old Harbor, like Anchorage, was rebuilt.

The village of Kaguyak was mostly destroyed not by the third but by the fourth wave. Kaguyak was not rebuilt but relocated. Survivors joined the village of Akhiok.

Half of Afognak collapsed in the earthquake, and the ground there sank several feet, putting much of the village below high tide line. Seventeen villagers voted to rebuild the village; eighteen voted to relocate. Ultimately, the village was relocated from Afognak Island to a new site on Kodiak Island and renamed. It is now Port Lions.

To rebuild is to start from the place. Remake what used to be right there, on the very same ground. But to relocate is to depart from the place. To relocate is to start from the idea. Relocation carries the memory of an idea to a new place, and the new place hatches that wise, resilient, tenacious idea back into the world. Continuity and discovery share, in relocation, common cause.

Patches of dead skin curl from my fingers like birch bark. I pretend I am a tree, a birch tree, to make the peeling of this hard outer layer normal. But I cannot account for the blisters. And the blisters are bursting. The newly exposed layer of skin ringing my knuckles is only a thin membrane between the inside of my hands and the outside. When I'm cold, the baby-new skin is purple. When I'm warm, it is salmonberry red. But the curled sheaves of dead skin peeling back are always yellow. Still attached, unresponsive to salves or creams, unresponsive to warmth; skin that doesn't seem to be part of my body at all.

For my body is well. I am a single cell of the whole cool, dark coast. My molecules are its molecules. I feel the correspondence all day as a persistent, perfect tingle the length of my spine. Now it is summer 2009, and this time I am kayaking through Southeast Alaska, the archipelago in which I was born.

Sometimes I sleep on beaches I slept on as a child, or maybe even on beaches where my mother and father honeymooned. But most nights, I discover new rocks on which to pitch my tent, find new tree limbs from which to suspend my food bags, listen to the topography for word of freshwater creeks, daily finding new icy streams over which I have never, not once, ever bent my head to drink. But the water is ancient in my mouth and meets my tongue with old recognition.

One-third of Chenegans died in the 1964 tsunami. Two-thirds survived and evacuated. Some began new lives in Anchorage. Others in Seattle. Most moved to Tatitlek, another village in Prince William Sound.

But Chenega wasn't rebuilt in that handful of years following the quake. In other words, no one returned to the old village site, at least not to live there.

Twenty years later, locals penned "New Chenega" on their maps, for a group of Chenegans created their own village again, afresh. They relocated to Crab Bay on Evans Island.

Odd interim, the two decades between earthquake and relocation.

The earth lurched, the wave came, the village was destroyed, and the island, never to be their home again, has also always remained their home. By what trick of fiscal policy, by what caprice of state and federal permitting, did the relocation take so long? By what pain in the spirit? By what design of the coastal forest organism itself?

The strangeness of these dead yellow curls, skin that seems not my own, reminds me of Old Chenega, of the summer I saw its silver schoolhouse on the knoll. I remember the rain pounding its certainty on the orange deck of my kayak, my neoprene gloves soaked and squishing with my grip on the paddle, blade pulling the sea over and over with something else's strength moving through my body. I remember how I kept my eyes on the silver beams of wood as I paddled, just fifteen minutes perhaps, along the arc of the beach along which there was once a village. I could not imagine a village back into being; the forested mountain island was steep and dark like every other one and that is what I saw: the island's steepness. Its dark trees. And up there, a knoll. The grass was hip high and bowing with gusts of wind, smacking against old beams of exposed lumber.

Sometimes my eyes fly open and I realize they have been clenched shut against the heat of infection, that I have been navigating not by the mountains or the shoreline but by the bone-colored lights splashing inside my eyelids. Sometimes I realize I have been paddling, weeping.

If the earth shudders and buildings crumble, someone in the city must dispatch the Coast Guard. Someone must fly over regional villages, check on them. So it went that the initial Coast Guard flyover of Chenega occurred right after the quake—but yielded no report of damage. The village was so cleanly absent that the pilot, new to the area, noted no distress. Absent wreckage, absent debris, the pilot saw just a friendly

97

gesture from a few people up on the knoll. He circled once, banked east and north, and flew back to Anchorage.

Not that an inexperienced pilot chose blindness or elected to misunderstand survivors' waving arms as a "friendly gesture." But sight nevertheless emerges here as a skill, a sensitivity gained in part by being steeped in a particular world, and also in part through practice, for often one must practice seeing—really seeing—what rests in plain sight.

Only when the mail plane arrived the next day did anyone from outside the village realize Chenega Island had changed. This is what the mailman saw: seventy feet of clean mountainside. And so he filed a report. *Gone village*. Chenegan survivors had spent the night on the side of the mountain in the forest. Now they evacuated, leaving their island, leaving home. The island beneath their feet was not safe. But it was their island.

As the burning in my hands makes bone-colored lights inside my eyelids, I think of taking as beloved something that will never make me a promise, and to which I am devoted regardless. I think, *I am not the first*.

In 1867 Russians decimate the sea otters for their pelts, then sell Alaska to the United States. A century later, in 1968, someone strikes oil on the North Slope in Prudhoe Bay, yielding two imperatives.

The first is to build an eight-hundred-mile oil pipeline from the North Slope down to the port of Valdez in Prince William Sound.

But the second imperative takes precedence over the first. The second imperative is to settle aboriginal land claims—thus delineating the terms of Alaska land ownership—so that an eight-hundred-mile pipeline can be built north to south from the Arctic plains, through the tundra, into the boreal forest, all the way to the coastal rainforest where old-growth tree limbs reach out over the rocks.

The legal solution passes in 1971, when the federal government and the State of Alaska agree on the Alaska Native Claims Settlement Act (ANCSA). ANCSA grants Native Alaskans a cash settlement and a land settlement. It organizes tribes into for-profit, landholding corporations. The Native corporations are charged with managing their lands for the financial profit of their shareholders. They are to do this by "developing" their "surface resources." The people are thus to assimilate into a capitalist cash economy. The land is thus to assimilate into the same.

About placing the land in for-profit corporate hands? Perhaps the organism doesn't care, doesn't register it, exists on a plane too far removed. Or perhaps the organism's seething makes so low a sound the young people are born breathing it, exhaling something of its rage every step of their lives. I don't know. But I suspect. I have begun listening for these tones.

I sift through memories every day: childhood field trips to Juneau's Alaska State Museum for "Indian Studies." Many of my classmates were white, many were Tlingit, and many were Filipino. We'd file into the museum wearing the paper headdresses we'd colored and stapled earlier in the day and receive small cardboard boats packed with potlach food. I remember we were embarrassed by the paper cut-out headdresses. I remember we ate the frozen blueberries from our potlach dishes but refused the rest of the food. I remember waiting for the field trip to end, looking away from the white cardboard boats of food piling up in the trash. It was painful then, yes, but it is more painful looking back. I know now but did not know then that some kids were poor. Had surely come to school without breakfast. And I did not know then that some kids had grandmothers who sewed and wove and carved and beaded those same designs about which we children felt shame. That some grandmothers felt the shame too. Shame, pride, ancestry, conviction—all balled up. And I didn't understand how the kids, all of us, all together, were teaching each other it was better to go without lunch than to eat Native food, how this warped us across ethnicity, across skin color, across heritage. Still, it must have been hardest on the kids who hadn't had breakfast.

Also, I didn't know some kids had grandmothers who wept at their own corporations' logging projects, feeling the violence to the forest in the heat of their own wombs. And I didn't know that other kids had grandmothers who believed those trees should be cut, and their sons should grow rich in this new society that had migrated onto the land.

I did know that a Native corporation owned rights to the back side of my own island, Douglas. I did know the grown-ups spoke of the corp in hushed tones, fearful of that corp's negotiations with the logging industry. So I knew to be afraid of Native corporations, but I did not know the underbelly of forces pulling and pushing actual Native people. I think now that such experiences created a hardened place in me, a trained avoidance demanding concerted work—every day—to counteract.

Chenega in the moment of the quake: the land undulates, becomes liquid beneath sprinting feet. The sea pulls back in one sharp breath and the tide is low, lower than it has ever been. On the exhale, a seventy-foot wall of water takes down a swath of forest and the village built within it.

The water would not really have arrived as a wall. It is the architecture of my own fixation that yearns for such sturdiness. No, the water would have rolled, piled upon itself, unfurled in a great curve.

Thirty-one Chenegans perished in the wave.

Sixty-three Chenegans departed on the day of the evacuation.

Twenty years later, a group of them reconvened and live once again in a village of their own.

Sure, some of the money moving around in 1971, when ANCSA was signed, is funneled into plans to rebuild a new village for Chenegans. But it takes thirteen more years for the gears of this project to mesh and turn.

Chenegans, meanwhile. Are their lives made of waiting? Perhaps waiting is simply the force of a muscle tensing, each fiber drawing nearer to its neighbor, hugging the bone, until the moment arrives for a leap, a sprint. A shudder.

I take antibiotics for a staph infection because this is the medication in my kit. But the infection is not staph, and these pills won't stymie it. What they will do is kill my strength; as my digestive flora withers, the food I eat feeds my body less and less.

Still, I spend my days on the water paddling and my nights in a synthetic bag sheltered by a tent the color of lupines. It is often raining, always cold. Alpine glaciers crouch atop mountains; tidewater glaciers tongue the sea. My surest instinct is that ice will heal my hands, that rain will choke the fire, that the organism is safety incarnate. My consciousness and body are two simple threads in its weave, and I still think that is a viable definition of love.

This is the historic account espoused in 2001 by economic report-writers:

The Natives enrolled in the Chenega Corporation
selected their new village site at Crab Bay on Evans
Island in the Prince William Sound in March of 1977.
The Chenega Corporation and the Chenega IRA
(Indian Reorganization Act) Council worked together
to obtain funding for roads, a water and sewer system, electric generators, a boat and floatplane dock,
and a school. The new village named Chenega Bay
was finally occupied in 1984 following the construction of 21 Housing and Urban Development (HUD)
homes.

What was it like for Chenegans to live in Tatitlek?

Anthropologists write about the church choir. When
Chenegans come to live in Tatitlek, when the two villages fold
together, what they do is sing. There are enough voices, enough
vocal ranges, enough hands to turn pages, enough bodies to
fill the risers. Enough to carry the melody and enough to har-
monize. The church in Tatitlek has a blue onion dome on top.
It is much lighter than the trees around it, surprising in the
forest and thus visible from a great distance, even before the
harbor comes into view.

After twenty years, does moving into HUD housing on
Evans Island feel like going home?

One day in the future, hands healed, unblistered, I will gaze
out from behind a window and wonder if I made a choice or if
I was swept along. It will be odd to sit warm and dry indoors
looking out, both nestled in the organism's fold and yet separated from it by a pane of glass. I will feel great longing, for
indoors, the light from the fixture is not rightly the organism's

light. The air from the vents is not rightly the organism's air. I will look out through glass panes at the silver rain, the steep mountain, and ask, going indoors, is this giving up? Is it necessity? Did I go indoors myself, as if solving a problem? Did the organism displace me? And what if it did? Then the overwhelming question: do I still share the ancient molecules of the cool, dark coast—that is, do I belong to it, and it to me? (Several notes will sound at once.)

When finally the new site on Evans Island yields an actual village, when finally Chenegans live there together again, the children only know of the earthquake as a story. Those who ran from the wave, whose mothers and fathers held them close for warmth that night on the mountainside, they are grown. They have children of their own.

In my imagination, hands grasp new doorknobs and pull. The doors are stiff against thresholds freshly pounded into place, not yet settled. I imagine a flip of the light switch, a pause, and steps gingerly taken across empty floors.

I stash my kayak above high tide line on a beach near one end of a small town's road system. I bushwhack up the hill to the road and walk along the shoulder until I have occasion to put out my thumb. I climb into a black pickup, cluttered bench seat smelling of sawdust. The driver takes me to the health clinic, dropping me at its entrance. The automatic door slides open, pulling in chill air along with my body and sealing behind me.

A nurse swabs my burst blisters, prepares a culture for the lab, writes a prescription, and recommends rest. We speak to one another candidly. I live out of a kayak and sleep in a tent. My life is cold and wet and the nurse suggests I reassess it.

Chenegans' vision of a new, relocated village comes to fruition because of oil money. The coastal forest organism watches through slitted eyes. Five short years later, the *Exxon Valdez* oil spill poisons Chenegans' hunting, fishing, and gathering grounds. The extractive industrial machine that funds the village's relocation also strands it, subsistence severed from place, community cleaved from sea, rock, and air.

Or perhaps the spill happens because of a song.

Oil tankers arrive and depart, navigating Valdez Arm, the Valdez Narrows, the Port of Valdez, its tides and blizzards and the rafts of icebergs off the Columbia Glacier, a mile long at its face, calving day and night into the sea. When wind and tide and calving conspire, entering Valdez Arm is tricky business. Leaving it is too.

Because ice clogged the tanker's charted route the night before Good Friday of 1989, the captain asked for and received Coast Guard permission to move from the outbound tanker lane to the inbound tanker lane. He swung the *Exxon Valdez* due south. The tanker passed into the charted lanes and then out of them. Shortly before midnight, the captain turned in, went to bed.

Soon after, the ship's lookout reported the flashing red light of Bligh Reef off the starboard bow. In safe waters, the light would have been off the port side of the ship. The third mate tried to take corrective action. The chief mate pounded on the second mate's door just after midnight: *Vessel aground. We're fucked.* About a half hour after midnight the captain radioed the Coast Guard: *We've fetched up hard aground. Evidently we're leaking some oil, and we're going to be here for a while.*

In a culture that demands martyrs and scapegoats and fixates on assigning guilt and hanging the banner of fault, the disaster washes through public consciousness in two waves. First, there is individuated blame set upon the captain on

104

one hand and the company on the other. Second, there is systemic blame, placed squarely on the shoulders of corporate, extractive culture. That is, on the fossil fuel economy underpinning most recognizable features of the global present.

Six or eight years after the skin on my hands has healed, I meet an unexpected oil spill historian—David Grimes, a prominent figure in the spill response and ensuing clean-up efforts. Unexpected, because we meet by accident at a gravel parking lot in the hardwood forests of midcontinent America, where our matching Alaska license plates are both a surprise and a sign. We become friends.

These days, David and I meet for a hike now and again. He tells me about his molecules, how they're aligned with the Sound, how the biome he calls the organism choreographed everything—the spill, the outcry, the clean-up, even the lingering damage to itself. He says the molecules that are "him" are the molecules of that organism, and I gather he sees his life's actions dictated not by an agency of his own but rather by a larger one, an agency of the earth. It is the story of his life. He likes to tell it, and I like to hear it.

The organism, David suggests, is capable of anything. It created the spill because it had the courage to devise and swallow a dangerous medicine, one bordering on poison. The spill, reframed in this way, transcends human accident and becomes a sick and exquisite sacrifice on the part of the biome itself.

As I ponder this idea and reimagine the disaster I hear a low thrum, a sound that is a song. *Swing low, sweet chariot,* moans the organism as its own ice, its own winds, its own tides join their voices to a larger convergence, one luring the tanker onto the organism's own rocks, the ones marked on all the charts as Bligh Reef. The rocks receive the tanker delivered unto it, opening its inch-thick steel hull in a long gash on the altar of the sea.

Some jagged hunks of metal found afterward are the size of pickup trucks. Others are rolled into twisted tubes the size and length of human appendages. Eight of eleven cargo holds are ruptured, and oil rushes out so fast it is two feet higher than the sea around it, rolling and boiling about the grounded tanker. A thick black wave flows into the night, and because the response vessel is out of operation, there will be no attempt to stanch the flow for several days. Then a storm will arrive, breaking the slick into three parts: one that reaches proximate beaches, suffocating 1,300 miles of coastline; one that sails across the surface of the sea, eventually reaching the village of Chignik on the Alaska Peninsula 460 miles away; and one that sinks to smother the seafloor.

The organism will either die of the cure or survive it. *Swing low, sweet chariot, coming for to carry me home.*

Good Friday mourns Christianity's most somber moment, the crucifixion. Churches silence their organs and bells so that only desolate chanting emanates from within.

During the Good Friday quake of '64 the shuddering earth and surging water must have sounded equally dense, equally guttural.

And the quake's twenty-fifth anniversary marked perhaps the organism's own most somber moment. The *Exxon Valdez* hemorrhaged on Bligh Reef the day of Chenega's most acute mourning and would not be stanched. The oiled sea, the coated beaches, the days and the weeks and finally the two months of crude oil spreading, smothering, saturating—all this in grim mimicry of Good Friday shrouding practices, for traditional Catholics wear black and drape a dark purple cloth over crucifixes, portraits, statues, and mirrors.

Purple is penance. Black is death. Crude oil is sheer density, the rainbow collapsed.

The cure. A perverse angle, perhaps.

My molecules are its molecules: the words belong to David Grimes, the unexpected historian. And I find myself repeating his phrase at odd moments. I see a toddler, following with her eyes a small army of songbirds—twisting in the arms of an uninterested father who hasn't noticed the flitting and chittering, which troubles me. *My molecules are its molecules.* But with whose molecules do I identify? The toddler's? The birds'? All the molecules of the moment, perhaps. The girl's molecules are the molecules of trying to see something evasive and plain, dirt-colored. And there are the molecules of her father's not noticing. And the molecules of the birds' busy flitting, their winged lives.

This is what the unexpected historian meant: his molecules are the organism's. He is aligned with the intelligence of a system he can't see completely; in time and space its scope exceeds him. *My molecules are its molecules,* he said. *I'm in its current. It does what it does.*

In saying so, he finds a rhythm. His story is a pulse.

We worked without rest to clean the spill, he says, remembering the eighties, the nineties. *The earth organism choreographed it. The spill, and also our myopic response. Lives were lost; lives were ruined. So when the logging industry came in with plans to clearcut we had to stand up, had to refuse. Maybe it's twisted, but our ruined lives were a defense. Of the organism's devising. Because once our grief bottomed out, no battle was too much. The organism could heal from an oil disaster—with deep scars. A steep price. But what it needed—it needed us to stop the clearcutting. And we did.*

How did it know. How did it know it could survive the oil.

Who can say. A gamble. But it knew logging was a nail in the coffin. The organism learned. Oregon demolished. Washington too. British Columbia alive but suffering. Southeast Alaska still strong but wounded, wounded.

So molecules align. I'm made of its molecules. The others were too. The intelligence, though—that's on another scale. It's large, large.

What happens, really, if we take the intelligence of the system as a ruthlessly creative force? We wake to odd debts, both roused into liveliness and pierced by loss.

The unexpected historian appears here and there throughout the spill literature. In one history of the spill, fisherman, scientist, and leading activist Ricki Ott invokes David Grimes's voice at a pivotal moment in the early days of devastation: *When there's nothing you can do, you're freed from limitations. You can go for it.* His attitude crystallizes what Ott calls "the emboldening heart of the crisis response." His adulthood unfolds on the front lines of local activism reacting first to the spill, next to Exxon's stupendous and warping legal campaign, and later to the Eyak Corporation's logging plans.

A map of the spill features neat curves, each labeled with a terse remark on the weather system that built, arrived, and then spread the oil slick eleven thousand square miles over two months. It is the curve of day four that shows oil coating what Chenegans hold dear. It is the curve of day four that indicates a poison slick upon the water, toxic fumes in the air, and a crude sludge sinking into beaches, into shellfish beds. Overnight, there is no hunting. No fishing. No foraging for sea asparagus, no pause for a slow lungful of sea air pulled deep inside the ribs. Someone distributes face masks.

108

The summer I am sick, I eventually receive word from the lab, receive new antibiotics. This species of infection is often enough fatal, but then again, it is an infection usually contracted only by those already nearing death. I am supposed to be the opposite. Alive with vitality far beyond my own body. In step, in swing. Evidence: one horizonless day on glassy gray water a loon locks its red eyes with mine, our courtship a funnel into which we both plummet. Slice of paddle blade, swoop of seabird. The loon stitches and dives from this side of my kayak to that, spreading his wings each time he surfaces to beat away the space between us, throat shuddering with seduction and regret. Autonomy is out of the question. I belong to him in full, our union witnessed by the gray mirror of the sea, ordained by the gray depth of the sky.

Still, doctors agree with the nurse who first received the lab results. Get immediate and aggressive treatment, they say. Live with the costs of the cure.

I refuse for a time. Then something gives. I am hauled out of the backcountry and wedged into my childhood bed, too weak to consider the costs of the cure until later. For now, the cure is not so bad. "Aggressive treatment" does not demand amputation or organ transplant or anything else worth reporting. A shift in antibiotics, expensive but acquired affordably through a special arrangement, a loophole maybe. Four or five weeks of medication, followed by another eight weeks to recover from the medication. It is a time of dream-horrors. I cannot stay awake. I sleep all day. Press my hot cheek to the porcelain of the bathroom sink. I am made of wood. My limbs are too heavy to lift, my eyes too tired to see through glass. But about six weeks in my body grasps at some conviction— which I still hold—that it is never quite right to be enclosed.

By power not my own I step out the back door into the forest but am too weak to amble more than a minute or two. Even so, it is good to be free, trail underfoot, spiderwebs eerie and alive on the skin of my face. I just stop as I need, sit, doze. The moss is thick and good. The sun is fresh and almost warm. The damp shade of the forest goes forever. *I'll just stay here*, I think. *I'll just stay here. Join the forest.* But a thrush interrupts, signaling with its one loud trill that I must move along.

You are, shouts the thrush, *a creature with arms and legs. Not a rooted thing. Not a rooted thing at all.* And the thrush, of course, is right.

THE GUT

When Rachel traveled for a holiday by the tropical sea, she hadn't the ambition to swim out past the breakers. She just sat down in the froth of the waves, plunk, and let the tumbling white of each crash drag her slight frame downbeach, push her back up, tug her sideways, and fill her pajama pants with sand. The French say *les vagues* for "the waves"—*vagues* like the English "vague" (as in "uncertainty" but also related to "vagabond," to "vagrant"), and I wonder now if my friend's minimalism in the surf was born of premonition, a sense she might appreciate—though never trust—*les belles vagues*. But at the time it was her glee that struck me: how satisfied she was with this salty edge, how all she needed was wave after wave sloshing into her lap and sucking sand from beneath her calves. The sea pulled and spun her, sure, but she wasn't even in deep enough for it to disturb the posture of her slender back.

French waves and English vagueness also share their name with a nerve, the vagus nerve. It's the one that wanders throughout the body. It livens the lungs. It animates the stomach. It is responsible for the ear canal, for sweating, for the rate at which the heart pumps grief and love over the body's crags and planes, into its crevices. But for all its wandering the vagus nerve always keeps a firm hand on the throat where it is gatekeeper of each gasp, each sigh, and every gulp or swallow.

One day Rachel phones to say she's planted a tree with her placenta. Her voice rushes along in my telephone. *Finally took care of that!*

She corrects herself: *Our* for her and her son. *Our placenta.*

I hadn't known Rachel was using a corner of her freezer to store her placenta. Their placenta.

But when she says she's planted it I imagine her standing, brushing dirt off her hands, a strand of hair having escaped from her ball cap. I see this with unexamined certainty—she's wearing her Carhartts and her turquoise plastic-rimmed glasses have slid a bit low on her nose.

It's quite clear. But also it isn't. Wouldn't there be blood? Things once-frozen, now-thawed, get drippy. In my mind I search for the blood. She inhales and releases one full breath into the receiver.

She is mindful, deliberate. Her posture is impeccable and she always remembers to breathe.

But every time she opens the freezer, she says, she's been seeing it and thinking she's *got to do something about that.*

I make noises that mean I am nodding. Her child is ten.

And she tells me the whole story, about putting the placenta in the freezer, intending to plant it, not getting around to it during various periods of life, then taking it out the other day, finding a place for it to thaw. Burying it. So now it's done, it's in there, in the tundra with all the mosses, the Labrador tea. She hopes the tree lives. She thinks it should; it's the right time of year to plant.

I can show you where she and I come from, even if you've never been, even if you'll never go. Or even if you've been there millennia longer than I. Make a cat paw of your right hand, palm down. The base of the fingers should remain rigid, you should have divots of skin unstretched where your knuckles on the back of your hand do not bend, but rather arch. The fingerpads tuck in tightly, pressed to the upper mound of your palm's flesh. Now extend only your index finger and your thumb—the remaining three fingers must stay tucked—and raise your elbow to swivel your hand, that you may study the shapes head-on. Everyone, in their right hand, carries this map of Alaska. Recently I've lived here and there, but I grew up in (and always return to) Juneau, on the bony upper segment of the thumb, a bit below the strong widening flesh of the palm. And Rachel lives much farther north, in Fairbanks, on the thinnest skin on the back of the hand where veins run close to the surface.

When it turns out I'm moving down south, to the heart of the contiguous forty-eight, we turn three thousand miles of interstates into four thousand miles of national parks and back roads. Eventually it's high summer in Missouri and we have never tasted air so heavy. She touches my arm, asks if I'm really going to stay, and returns north. I don't know anything about staying but I'm here at the moment, legs tucked against my chest, body wedged between white painted cabinets and the edge of the kitchen table as she plants her placenta in the tundra.

Other than hers, there is no mother whose birthing I wish I had seen. My friend's stretchmarks run dry in bone-colored creekbeds down her belly. Her belly, which is flat, which is white, which is more collapsed even than will be her voice.

I have neglected to mention, until now, that my friend is going to get her head cut open, and that it'll happen soon. She will fly to Seattle and a surgeon will remove a tumor from her middle ear. Maybe the cut will not sever the nerve that controls the flicks and shadows of her face. Maybe it will not interrupt her capacity to swallow. Maybe she will contract no hospital infections in the days they keep her under strictly monitored surveillance for postoperative seizures. Maybe the knife will not bump her brain, jar her personality. Maybe the scar will be very, very small, a pink teardrop behind her left earlobe, an opal purse hung from an ivory shoulder.

The northern rainforest of my childhood home is somber, green-black, the air alkaline from the sea and lightly bitter from the spruce needles. But where my friend left me, Missouri's middle continent summer is an oversweet, torpid green. Shoots curve under their own pulpy weight. Sunshine tunnels in, skates the undersides of certain ridged leaflets, a needle almost threading clarity but swallowed in shifting shades and shadows. Suspicious of air so thickened with heat and leaves, I keep watch through the kitchen window. It would take a wise plumber to knock sense into this kind of green, to wrench and tighten its pipes just so and contain the lush slop.

When I wade through to the edge of the property, there is a bit of barbed wire weighted down by the underbrush between a couple of hackberry and oak trees. Midday, people play golf on the other side of this wire, and mornings, other people groom the green in oblong patterns. But most of the time all this belongs to chiggers and raccoons, frogs and possums. Daytimes I work indoors, romping out on the green with the dog only at night when the owl hoots. It's a sound that thins the air to breathable. I find it takes, here as anywhere, a predator to clear some space.

I think of fixity, of people who stay put, of forces bound to their cycles and that in this sense stay put too. I think of the sea, the fjords I came from, and of the first people who got there by sliding under the blue belly of a glacier. How they came out from under the ice and then stayed, how now that is the way it has always been.

We can think back together. I recommend crouching. Stay low and steady in the bottom of the canoe—the one people paddled under the ice. When they reached the far side of the glacier and came out from under it, gray light pricked the pupils of their eyes and the sky placed its open hands to the tops of their heads, applying a weight that radiated the length of them, vertebra to vertebra, widening their chests like buoys. When they came out from under the ice, they became ocean people.

Blinking in the daylight and temporarily bowlegged from the new weight of outer space on their spines, the people disembarked. I don't know exactly where. On the bank of something rocky, I would guess, although I don't have all of the details. There was more than one ancient migration, after all.

If you're like me and you're forced to realize these are not your ancestors, stay crouched in the canoe, out of the way, because you are clumsy enough to warrant caution. Do not stand to see, do not try to step out onto the rocks. If you are so luckless as to tip the canoe into those wavelets teased up by the breeze, you will plunge into a piece of sea cold as a blade. And your body's reflex will be to gasp and gulp like a fish; you will fill your own lungs with seawater. The people may or may not notice although they would, as is often the case with association, bear responsibility for the brunt of your mistake.

What my lineage is not: Indigenous, aboriginal, First Nations, Native. Having arrived by way of a glacier. Bound by ancestors, art, cosmology, an act of Congress—to the northern end of the northern archipelago, *Lingít Aaní*.

What my lineage is: vagabonds. Migrant farmers and rabbis fleeing west over the ocean, Middle American children of administrators tempted still farther west over the continent, long-haired students of law picking their way north over forested rocks to the far end of the same archipelago, Southeast Alaska.

It is true that people slid beneath a mile of ice but I made up the part about the sky pressing down on them at the other side; I've never heard of human physiology figuring in to the start of time or the beginning of the world like this. I also made up the possibility that you could think yourself into the story, crouching low in the canoe as a sort of foolish stowaway during the world's inception. I don't know, offhand, how to get in on the old stories. I've had to improvise.

Barbara Kingsolver embedded herself decades ago in the Sonoran Desert but writes that she has yet to shed the deepest intuitions of her childhood home at the edge of a creek in Kentucky. She struggles to grow tomatoes in the drought-stricken hardpan of her strange backyard. Behind the howl of coyotes she still listens for meadowlarks.

I'm a northerner in the middle of Missouri—not Kentucky, but bordering it. I perch on the kitchen chair, knees drawn up to my shoulders, where it's a tight fit between the white painted cabinets and the edge of the table. I have to fold myself just right to huddle fully against the wall, and I have to stay there until I am stiff because it takes time for stillness to reach my body, to begin spreading from the wall into the folded length of me. The crosshatch of the window screen presses on my vision until my gaze slows to a combing free of hitch. I know what it's doing. My body is trying to look out over a distance of water that isn't there, to travel far away from the tangle of so many leaves, shoots, stems, petioles.

I imagine someone, anyone, Barbara Kingsolver even, with a heart full of this swollen greenery. Does she have to take nippers to her soul if she wants to clean out some space for a line of flight? Isn't having a straight shot at the open a necessary condition for departure?

Maybe not. Watch, study. It appears grass crevices are for darting (quick flick of garter snake), leafy tunnels for dodging (leap of gray squirrel). The open, then, is maybe more for the wanderers among us than for the seekers.

What I think about tumors: if unchecked growth—the yang of expansion absent the yin of contraction—is the ailment, and if the opposite is the antidote, of course Rachel and I turn toward things that ebb and flow, toward cycles, toward emptiness that yields replenishment. Of course she plants her placenta, but that is only the first gesture preceding intent, the thought before the thought. We know so little about the ailment. We plan the travel, the coming and going.

The day after the surgery I am to board three airplanes and four buses and meet my friend in Seattle, the city where she will have her head cut open. We speak rarely and briefly at best about facial paralysis or gradual starvation or brain damage, which are, alongside death, the most clinically pressing concerns. Instead, we worry the surgery will produce inalterable voice change and rehearse, for some reason, our attachment to her sound. I want to hear from her all the time. I want to *hear her* all the time.

What does an origin story do?

It remembers when a filament of reality tried threading some colorless path underground. Digging in? To set down roots of the world as it now is?

Perhaps.

In any case, as far as I can tell the world begins similarly in each telling of it, as a malleable thing, unfixed. And the world leaves off similarly in each telling as well, as a less malleable thing, a few notches closer to the one we live in.

Can't get there from here! What is that song even about? What is that song not about?

Here is the whole story.

Ringing in the head and a deafened left ear bring my friend to the ear doctor, who sees a small red spot in her ear canal; CT scans and MRIs suggest a glomus jugulare tumor. Her file changes hands and she becomes the responsibility of a surgeon at a major hospital down south. Once there, she undergoes a full anesthetic two days in a row. On Monday the surgeon cuts off the major blood vessels leading to the tumor. On Tuesday he goes in for the tumor itself. But he finds two, a littler one and a bigger one. The bigger one, he explains afterward, was a total mess, *just stuck to everything*, a growth on the nerve itself, working its way into the brain. But he gets it. He is forced to cut a nerve but he gets it, gets them both.

Tumors that, as he put it, were *benign* and *quite aggressive*. I have yet to resolve the dissonance.

That is the whole story but I'm thinking about it because the nerve, the one he cut, is the tenth. The vagus nerve.

Vague (adjective):
A state of uncertainty as to specifics

118

The word comes to us by way of the Middle French—*vague*, not waves, exactly, but empty, vacant, wild, uncultivated, wandering—and originally from the Latin *vagus*. Figuratively, *vagus* means vacillating, uncertain. Literally, the word is for strolling, rambling. One nerve's severance compromises my friend's voice, her capacity to swallow, her ability to register hunger. The point is that what was once animated by the force of the vagrant, the wanderer, now has to draw life from elsewhere.

Wedged in against the white painted cabinets and the edge of the table, I hold still in posture alone. I'm employed in the ninth job I've held since college and live in the third home I've occupied this year. I keep filing taxes marked "occupation: drifter." But I'm nothing special. Cowboys drift. So do Arctic explorers; they pack supplies in anticipation for their ships to get stuck in the winter ice, locked in as the sea currents push the ice floes. Maybe a lead will open up in the spring; if the ship's not been crushed they'll resume navigating. Whenever, wherever—it's a journey charted in grays, sort-ofs, maybes, free of path. And traceless, for ice shifts to close behind them. Or the ice shifts to close overhead, if they sink.

So I hold to the family that paddled out from under a glacier. Their descendants are a people who have long since stopped their wandering, who are as deeply at home as can be. I wonder if it is possible to learn something from this, from a story about people who have been established since myth-time, who learned to live off salmon that come and go, spawn and die, in such a rocky old-growth rainforest that the trees all grow on the fallen trunks of their progenitors—who learned to live, in other words, not of wandering forces but of cycling ones, forces that repeat, trace and retrace, echoing the echo.

The hospital, the surgeon's severance, those first days? They're behind us now, but also not. I study the overlay of green shadows, green air, shifting green humidity, but when my focus falters, when my mind won't still, again and again I am striding into the hospital in Seattle with plane-soured armpits. The front desk gives its rehearsed directions to the ICU and my rolling suitcase whirs unevenly the whole way. When I step into the unlit room, I naturally do not elect to register the dish of my friend's face upon the pillow.

I register screens and machines and poles and bars; the room is dark and *hold up ma'am!* Hold up because you wash your hands before coming into this room. Every time. And it's not clear how to wash my hands, where to wash my hands, where to leave my suitcase while I am washing my hands, why my hands, and should I step in a footbath to sanitize these feet that walked the dog through uncut grass in the Missouri night, that walked onto one plane and then off of it, onto another and then off of that one as well, feet that dragged a suitcase through Seattle summertime highs onto the light rail, off of the light rail, transfer station, sidewalk, bus . . . ?

But there's a squeezepump on the wall and the rule is you squeezepump fizz on your hands to kill what's living there, then you can come in. And here is my friend's father and he knows me and is standing to greet me and introduce me to her mother, the one we hope will keep it together, and it's so good to meet you and it's so good of you to be here and how was your trip and how was *your* trip—but like I said, it's quite dark in the room. And I fear I may not recognize this mother under the unflinching fluorescents out in the corridor. It's as I am curtaining off into this dim worry that I hear the littlest sound, little like a rivulet, like the thread of a stream gone all but underground. The dish upon the pillow is saying my name.

She's saying my name.

If you manage to step out of the canoe, hoping to catch sight of her there, you mustn't budge. Within mere lifetimes you will feel a prick at the base of your spine where a single drop of sweat dries, disappears. You may wonder if it was a tear, if your shoulder blade has sorrow. Pry it up to see. That's the blade that juts against the summer night sky, a sky bright with pooling dusks and dawns because during summertime in the north, night can't find its foothold. That's the blade that is a ridgeline still scarred by currents of ice. That's the scapula, the shield holding up the back of the heart and housing the lungs: the mountain beneath which grief runs in white veins through the bedrock.

It was a six-hour operation. The time of one tide, high to low. Twenty-seven stiches curve from above her left ear down toward her jawline and jut halfway over her neck in a straight shot across the throat. I never counted the stitches on her abdomen. I never dared. That sweet lovely belly.

While severing the tenth nerve and removing a section of it—the surgeon explained this with his thumb and forefinger squared around a make-believe segment of air, which he plucked from the space between us with a jerk of the wrist—and while carving a porthole in the dura mater (the sac that, heavy with brain and cerebrospinal fluid, lines the inside of the skull), the surgeon watched upward of a pint of blood flow from my friend.

I think of the salmon hatchery where I spent an afternoon in orange Grundéns, industrial-quality rubber bibs, drawing my knuckle razor up female salmon bellies and using the other fingers to scoop fish eggs into white buckets to my right, buckets periodically taken away and replaced by the worker who watched over my efforts, who accounted for my mistakes.

He was the first to put my teenaged hands to work inside a fish when he taught me to unzip pinks that day; all he probably said to me about the egg take was, *You might like it.*

Razor cut after razor cut, the seduction was in the play between precision and ease of motion, in the light resistance at the top of the cut that would then yield like butter. Packed tight between flaps of splayed bellyskin lay the eggs, their mass of tangy, swollen globes as orange as embers. Scooping them along the length of each fish, my fingers would comb past still-beating hearts, past pale-gray sacs of stomach, past livers rich like chocolate. I remember the fish were marvel-ously slippery inside, that I felt instantly wedded to them by the intensity of our touch—devoted, ordained.

But I also remember the high-power hoses we used at the end of the day to rinse fish blood from the floor, the splashing that soaked us head to foot, the long-handled brushes we used to scrub slime from the stainless steel chutes. The smell of fish was suddenly strong, then; our fatigue, wooden. What a mess we'd made handling just-dead fish all day, scooping through their viscera. What a mess.

Rachel, I think, is not a fish.

I cannot imagine her like this, inert, bleeding. Fearfully beautiful inside but, in the end, demanding clean-up. Later I will touch the purple speckles high near the bridge of her nose, bruises telling it all but straight: she must have been clamped down. This I cannot imagine either.

One of the tumors was headed right for the depths of Rachel's head and to get it out, the surgeon had to rip the bag that held her brain in its cerebrospinal fluid bath. The dura mater.

Having ripped the dura, he needed a patch. So the surgeon cut not only into my friend's ear but also into her belly. He got a bit of fat to stuff into the rip, to reseal the bag of spinal fluid in which floated her brain. The trick, of course, is that patches are delicate. This one wouldn't hold against the normal pressure of cerebrospinal fluid until the dura accepted the patch and grew into it, so my friend's production of spinal fluid had to be stymied. *Yes,* the surgeon would say, the piece of fat was meant to function *like a cork,* confirming what I couldn't quite get around to: that this tube here, the one siphoning off spinal fluid, keeping the levels one hair above livable, was doing so in order to stave off a breach in the new levee he'd built next to her brain.

I learn from a nurse that every six hours the body makes and remakes, in tidal replenishment, all of its spinal fluid. I do not ask what this volume is, but I notice the plastic pouch hanging low from one of the rolling silver poles by my friend's bed seems filled with water, with something as clear and easy and continual as rain pooling from rivulets on a windowpane.

When I was small, say on the brink of learning to write, I had another friend. Cassie. Her fearlessness was total. She would shove off on her sled headfirst. She'd sprint on graveled pavement. I wanted to keep up but was a year younger and always the one to falter. The hill looked too steep for sledding. The gravel rolled under my sneakers and I fell.

A leukemia came, beginning the time during which Cassie was often away. I made cards for her, which my dad and I mailed together at the Douglas P.O. When Cassie came home for her birthday, she raised her shirt to show me the pale blue and yellow tubes sticking in and out of her flat kid-chest. I studied the white medical tape securing these tubes to her pierced skin. We were solemn about this; gravitas was only natural. Then we played. I don't know if the medicinal smell I recall was chemical in nature or simply fresh gauze. Cassie left town again shortly after. I resumed card-making. Time passed until she died, but stopped there. She was six. I was five.

A moment to marvel at surfaces. See how a body of water will glint above depths, never tipping its hand. At present, Cassie remains six and fearless, while I remain five, hesitant at the top of a hill, unsteady running on gravel.

Netter's Clinical Anatomy is not, for me, an easy read, though I appreciate the stoicism of the language. I'm attempting to learn that the vagus nerve is responsible for such varied tasks as heart rate, gastrointestinal peristalsis, sweating, various muscle movements in the mouth—including speech (also involving the recurrent laryngeal nerve)—and keeping the larynx open for breathing with a muscle called the posterior cricoarytenoid, which is the only abductor of the vocal folds. I'm trying to understand how the vagus nerve also has some afferent fibers that innervate the inner (canal) portion of the outer ear via the auricular branch (also known as Alderman's nerve) and that part of the meninges are somewhere in this picture too. It is important to absorb this but I'm also—predictably—understanding it better when my mind wanders off. My mind prefers to concentrate on this: how *vagus* shares its taproot with *vagrant* and *vagabond*.

What's gone from my friend's body is the force of wandering. To live, what she has to learn is a new kind of fixity. Her larynx has to relearn how to voice itself. Her throat has to relearn to swallow. Her stomach has to relearn hunger, has to create and receive the sensation on its own. This is just a preliminary list; who knows what else will unspool. The point is that what was once animated by the wanderer has now to draw life from elsewhere.

It has to be possible. It has to be possible to find a peculiar strength in fixity, even. The people who paddled out from under a glacier—they have to have once been wanderers to end up under the ice like that. They have to have been people who struck out, shoved off, drifted. Seeking and eventually caught in the current that pulled them in swift necessity under the blue lip of ice. Can the fibers of a body absorb something from a mythology?

I think of that which is fixed—the symbiosis of my archipelago's biome and the canoeing family that peopled it—as if some key, for my friend, could be deduced from an instance of continuity emerging. And I spend my hours watching the strange midcontinental greenery as if in renunciation of my own instinct to wander, as if the body I press to the wall could one day yield an offering, a lump of sympathetic stillness.

I read somewhere there are songbirds midcontinent who like to nest in piles of sticks. I could do that, I think: make big piles of sticks, beat back the green surge into brittle bonelike mounds. Coax in the thing with feathers, that armies of it may come and go.

So I ought to admit to the swallows. I dreamed them here, before my friend lost her body's wanderer. I dreamed swallows swooping among the piers of the wharf attached to the house by the side of the sea in Missouri, the one in which I now live.

In the dream the house is empty, it needs living in, and I fake nonchalance but I want to see it. I've passed a park with the close-in feel of continental town life, water tower visible in the middle distance. An Osage orange on the sidewalk. Pleasant, frank people who say *good morning*, all three syllables of it, as they pass. So I know while I am dreaming that this is no dreamscape: it's the straight-up Middle West of America. But in the dream the front door of the house is open and the wood floors are smooth and clean and empty and I fly through the air to the back, stepping out onto sturdy planks that are not a porch but a pier, not a deck but a dock, not a patio but a wharf built upon pilings that jut up from among barnacled rocks, pilings about which swallows dive and swoop as the tide permits.

And the sea sloshing just then against the pilings? It is open ocean, really, and goes to the horizon. When I lean over the railing, I can look straight down through the heaving seawater at the black rocks on which the pilings are set. Someone's painted rough marks along the rocks, indicating the best path to scramble down them at low tide.

So that's it; that's the whole thing. I dreamed there was a house in Missouri that looked out over the ocean. Waking, I moved into that house, the same one, blue in real life as in the dream. But in real life there's no horizon out back, no point at which the sky forces the sea to curve with the earth. Still, I painted the downstairs bedroom gray and white. Ship colors.

Anyway, there's no parsing the yard from the rolling tide of the golf course; the green carries on, full of froth and scum. Ferns curl against the house, obscuring the kitchen door. Shooting up overnight appear thistles covered in rows of spiny teeth like the jaws of those fish dwelling in the lightless deep, baiting in prey with the glow of a single firefly. Domesticated irises make leaves like wooden paddles that beat on the foundation during thunderstorms. What's the rush, I wonder. Does low tide never come?

Still, I can't help but look for swallows under the pier when I sip the air, testing it for the scent of tar that saturates all true seaside pilings. And nights when the wind kicks up, I listen for the boom of ocean waves clapping those black rocks.

Rachel wants us to have champagne. It's going to be the first anniversary of her body's fixity, the severance of its wanderer twelve months behind us. We each travel to my hometown in Southeast Alaska, meet in Juneau, and retreat together to Douglas Island where I grew up, where a glacier is visible across the channel on clear days but muted for now. Reassuring, still, to know the ice is nearby, just hidden by a soft gray sky, quieted by a soft gray drizzle. The air is cold and wet and so clean it cuts.

I pop the cork.

My friend holds the champagne flutes.

The first splashes of poured champagne send their quick frothy columns up to the lip of each glass. The froth peaks out over the edge, domes, recedes. I pause, but keep pouring— slowly though the bubbles make my friend laugh, make her glass an unsteady target.

Barely raining at all, we agree, barely even misting. We'll sit outside. We layer up, drag the deck furniture toward the shelter of the house, try to lean as much of our bodies as we can under cover of the eaves. We secure even the top button of our plaid wool shirts and nestle in. Watch our chilled fingertips grow white against the stems of our glasses. Watch the mist.

And while bubbles escape up so many strings through the champagne the air around us is alive with mute movement of its own, filled with zany silver specks of mist darting every which way. We sip, and those wild specks crash upon our bodies, shipwrecking there, collecting.

Eventually, the trapped mist grows visible along our shoulders, tracing the mat of fine hairs that hovers from the wool flannel of our shirts. Where many such hairs converge or cross, white specks meet one another and bead up into perfect droplets. These gradually swell until they begin, one by one, soaking into the fabric.

NOTES

The map in the hand replies to Joni Tevis's *The Wet Collection*, in which we find out the Carolinas are drawn in the seams of our palms.

"I have neglected to mention . . ." comes from Lia Purpura's *I have not yet said that all this is occurring while a friend back home is dying. And that her dying is a hand upon it, a breath upon it and a frame.*

Wide-chested ocean people is an image that came to me by way of Sherman Alexie. Can it be Thomas Builds-the-Fire who voices the notion that his people, fishermen, are Indians with bodies shaped by the sea?

Barbara Kingsolver, who still listens for meadowlarks behind the howl of coyotes, does so in her essay called "High Tide in Tucson."

"The thought before the thought." I have a feeling that's Maurice Blanchot, *The Writing of the Disaster*. And the "line of flight" is the unbounded movement Gilles Deleuze and Félix Guattari find in the rhizome they celebrate in *A Thousand Plateaus*.

The formula, "what is *x* about? What is *x* not about?" comes from John McPhee's *has any other writer ever done that? Has any other writer ever not done that?* He asks this question in his essay, "Draft No. 4: On the Writing Process."

My grasp of brain science is pretty shaky. I am most indebted to *Netter's Clinical Anatomy* because of its top-notch medical illustrations and thus owe special thanks to artists Frank H. Netter and Carlos Machado, both MDs. I alone am to blame for any misinterpretations of their artistry or of the text printed alongside it.

ACKNOWLEDGMENTS

It is an honor to think and live in northern places and it is an honor to write among transformative people.

Foundational thanks to Pomona professors N. Ann Davis, Oona Eisenstadt, Darryl Smith, and John Seery. I thought it over and as far as I can see, you are the reason I make essays.

Thank you to Daryl Farmer, Julija Šukys, and Michael White—all three writers, professors, and professors of writing. I learned things from you that made this collection possible.

Thank you to core readers Angie Netro, Travis Scholl, Eric Scott, Allison Coffelt, Leanna Petronella, and Caroline Crew.

Thank you to editor Peggy Shumaker for your guidance, to editor Nate Bauer, and to the staff of University of Alaska Press.

Appreciation every day for my expansive family. Thank you to my loving smart eccentric exuberant parents Tam and Greg. And to the lifelong friends you gathered as my aunts and uncles. And to my more than human family Number Seven, Spark, Scamper, Kimi, Hibou, and Moxie. Especially tender recognition to Pepper, my closest companion in the making of every sentence in this book.

In memory of P
Completely perfect, completely beloved
You stay with me; I stay with you.